PRAISE FOR
THE DAY I DIED

The Day I Died is a moving testament as to how relationships—
with ourselves, our families and friends, and even perfect
strangers are the source of our greatest strength in times of
need and our greatest joy in times of peace. If you take to heart
what Steve learned from the day he died, you'll someday be
writing your own book called *The Day I Lived!*

Keith Ferrazzi
Best-Selling Author, *Never Eat Alone: And Other Secrets to Success,
One Relationship at a Time*

The Day I Died is a needed book for this fast-paced world.
I recommend that anyone who is truly seeking God's balance in
his or her life should read it. Steve has an amazing story to tell
and he tells it in a captivating way. I actually read this book in
one sitting! Such honesty about real life is very refreshing.

Stephen LeBlanc
Senior Pastor, Trinity Fellowship
Amarillo, Texas

Steve Sjogren has been one of America's most influential pastors over the past decade. He has inspired tens of thousands of laypeople to reach out beyond themselves and connect disconnected people with Christ. His testimony is powerful and will encourage individuals to reflect on eternal questions. I am grateful for Steve's huge contribution to the contemporary church scene.

Rich Nathan
Senior Pastor, Vineyard Christian Church of Columbus
Author, *Empowered Evangelicals* and *Who Is My Enemy?*
Welcoming People the Church Rejects

If you can read only one book this year, make this the one. This may be the most uncompromisingly honest book that I have ever read.

Leonard Sweet
Drew University
George Fox Evangelical Seminary

Religious people, beware! Reading Steve Sjogren's *The Day I Died* could penetrate your pious ozones. There's no pulling of punches here, no apologies for the supernatural, no denying that God still speaks today, and no religious gobbledygook. Steve takes us into the hospital room where he died and went out into the world of post-death living. With characteristic Sjogrenian humor and warmth, Steve shares the insights and wisdom he gleaned after his near-fatal experience about vital life issues, such as the priorities of friends, relationships with our spouses and children, showing hospitality to strangers, and a dozen other issues of significance to us all. As I read his words, I laughed out loud, cried and repented. As you read this book, prepare to be changed.

Berten Waggoner
National Director
Vineyard Churches USA

Steve Sjogren has given us all a wonderful faith-filled testament of how to deal with the quality of life changes that come into our life, often unexpectedly. In doing so, Steve forces us to rethink the maddening pace that often keeps us from experiencing the true quality of life we find in God.

Robert Webber
Myers Professor of Ministry
Northern Seminary

Steve Sjogren

THE
DAY
I
DIED

BETHANYHOUSE

a division of Baker Publishing Group
Minneapolis, Minnesota

© 2006 by Steve Sjogren

Published by Bethany House Publishers
11400 Hampshire Avenue South
Bloomington, Minnesota 55438
www.bethanyhouse.com

Bethany House Publishers is a division of
Baker Publishing Group, Grand Rapids, Michigan

Bethany House edition published 2014
ISBN 978-0-7642-1589-6

Previously published by Regal Books

The Library of Congress has cataloged the original edition as follows:
Sjogren, Steve
     The day I died / Steve Sjogren.
        p. cm.
     Includes bibliographical references (p.   ).
     ISBN 0-8307-3812-6 (trade paper)
     1. Sjogren, Steve 2. Evangelists—United States—Biography. 3. Brain damage—
Patients—Biography. I. Title.
BV3785.S5117A3 2006
269'.2092—dc22   2005033233

All Scripture quotations, unless otherwise indicated, are paraphrased by the author. The
chapter and verse for each quotation cited is listed in the endnotes.

Scripture quotations labeled THE MESSAGE are from The Message by Eugene H. Peterson,
copyright © 1993, 1994, 1995, 2000, 2001, 2002. Used by permission of NavPress Publishing Group. All rights reserved.

Scripture quotations labeled NIV are from the Holy Bible, New International Version®.
NIV®. Copyright © 1973, 1978, 1984 by Biblica, Inc.™ Used by permission of Zondervan.
All rights reserved worldwide. www.zondervan.com

20   21   22   23   24   13   12   11   10

DEDICATION

This book is dedicated to my best friend, Dr. Osborne
Richards, senior pastor of New Life Outreach Church.
Your church is an amazing place that is changing lives every
day of the year. When I was in the hospital and so depressed
and out of it, I asked that no one come to visit me.
But you came every single day with a big smile on your
face and acted as if I had said nothing. You prayed for me
to be made well by God's power. Thank you for not
listening to me! I am better because of it.

CONTENTS

Foreword 11

Chapter One 15
A Beautiful Day to Die

Chapter Two 23
Dying for a Miracle

Chapter Three 33
Dancing at Death's Door

Chapter Four 43
Dying to Become a Turtle

Chapter Five 53
Dying to Be Normal

Chapter Six 65
Dying to Let Go

Chapter Seven 79
Dying to Be a Better Husband

Chapter Eight 93
Dying to Be a Better Father

Chapter Nine 103
Dying to Be a Better Friend

Chapter Ten 113
Dying to Be Even Kinder

Chapter Eleven 125
Dying to Be a Better Neighbor

Chapter Twelve 133
Dying to Know What to Say

Chapter Thirteen 139
Dying to Live to 90

Epilogue 151
Since the Day I Died

Postscript 155
The Day Terri Schiavo Died

Thanks. 165

FOREWORD

Everybody wants to have at least a hint about life after death—something like a movie preview would be nice. We know that there must be more; we just can't conceive of what it might be. Steve Sjogren got a glimpse the hard way. During and after his devastating medical accident, he discovered, as he reveals in this book, something we all want to know: How does death relate to *life*?

I have enjoyed friendship with Steve for 25 years. During this time, I have seen live and in person the before-and-after pictures. Steve's story gives us a sneak-peek into questions such as, Can we be alive apart from our body? What does non-bodied existence feel like? Is it *safe*? Is it *secure*? Are we aware of life going on around us? Does *personhood* really depend on *matter*—flesh, blood, heart and brain? What about the big scary thing: GOD? When we die, do we sense or know a supreme being's presence?

If what Steve discovered is true for all of us, then the material world indeed does depend upon something *even more real*—God—for its existence. This God is perfectly capable of being our God, and He doesn't have a physical gallbladder, brain or heart. He is a spiritual, non-embodied, personal

Reality—the *most real thing* in the world.

Steve didn't make this breakthrough the way scientists would discover something through experimentation or the way monks would reach a deeper level of understanding through prayer. He learned it the way that key lessons in life often come: His accident mugged and bag-snatched his previous worldview. No one chooses to go through a painful crisis. However, it is consistently true that people who face near-death or death-with-resuscitation experiences come out the other side as wiser people.

How does experiencing near-death change a person? Here is one possibility: What if in death we are not isolated from the world but see it *as it actually is*? Paul, who wrote much of the New Testament, gave us memorable words in 1 Corinthians 13 (called the "love passage") that are often quoted at weddings. You have probably heard them: "Love is patient, love is kind . . ." (v. 4, *NIV*). What is less known, but equally important, comes later in that passage:

We don't yet see things clearly. We're squinting in a fog, peering through a mist. But it won't be long before the weather clears and the sun shines bright! We'll see it all then, see it as clearly as God sees us (v. 12, *THE MESSAGE*).

Paul was referring to the revelation of God that will come to everyone either in life or in death. This breakthrough into clearness is the backhanded gift Steve was given. In death he saw things *as they are*. He witnessed what was *really going on*. This is true because, being made in God's image, we are not human beings having an occasional *spiritual* experience; rather, we are *spiritual beings* having a temporary human experience. Steve, as his spirit left his body, got in contact with Reality in a new and profound way. It changed him, and reading about his journey will change you as well.

I have a recurring thought that hit me again while reading *The Day I Died*. Evangelists—me included—often ask, "If you died tonight, where would you go [meaning heaven or hell]?" I wonder, if one were seeking to align his or her day-to-day life with Reality in the way that Steve describes it, if it would be more valuable to ask life-based questions such as: What if you knew you were going to live tomorrow—and in fact for a long, long time—what would you do differently? What if you knew you were going to live forever? Who would you follow? From whom would you learn to do life? Around what or who would you organize the daily activities of your life?

Bicyclist Lance Armstrong's yellow bracelets encourage us to "LiveStrong." To do so requires the assurance that we are safe and sound throughout time and eternity—whether in the body or out. From the new angle that God, the cosmos and each of us are more real in death, not less, Steve shares his inspiring and life-shaping message. He shows us how to trust and follow God in life and to do it in such a way that the people around us will experience it as humble grace and for their good.

Todd Hunter
Executive Director
Alpha USA

CHAPTER 1

A BEAUTIFUL DAY TO DIE

Today is a magnificent early winter day. It's crisp outside and the squirrels in my backyard are chasing one another through a big hollow tree. The red ones run after the less aggressive grey ones. Without a care in the world, they never seem to tire. It's great entertainment—better than satellite TV!

It's hard to believe that just a few years ago, on a day just as lovely as this one, all hell was about to break loose in a small suburban hospital just up the road. It's even harder to believe that I was the one on an operating table and the object of this life-and-death struggle.

Doctors had previously repaired my knees—both of them. Although those incisions were painful, they were necessary and rather anti-climatic. Now it was time to remove my gall bladder, but this surgery seemed to have a pall about it. For days leading up to what would turn out to be the ugliest day of my life, I had worried about my impending hospital visit. Something just seemed wrong. I had even considered taking a magic marker and writing TAKE OUT GALL BLADDER ONLY across my abdominal area. I didn't want the surgeon to mistake me for the guy who was due for a leg amputation.

A Strange Feeling

As a rule, I am allergic to mornings, but the early hours the day of my surgery were worse than usual. As my wife, Janie, drove me the few miles from our house to the hospital, I felt strangely sick to my stomach. As we got closer, I had second, third and fourth thoughts about going through with the surgery. Deep down, I must have realized that I hadn't done my homework about the risks of the operation, the surgeon's record or the hospital's reputation. I know better now—but I'm getting ahead of myself.

When we arrived at the hospital, I was still having hyper-heebie-jeebies. What was this ominous foreboding I sensed? The doctor seemed to be unexplainably anxious and seriously overwhelmed. The nurses acted as if they were besieged. Much of the equipment appeared to be malfunctioning—and there was only one-ply toilet paper in the bathroom! Call me loony, but in my book, that kind of bad mojo counts for something.

One particular nurse, detecting that I was unusually nervous, gave me a sedative. The medication sent me into la-la land. Soon I wasn't worrying or objecting to anything. All foreboding vanished and my attitude changed to "bring it on." While the doctor and nurses made their final preparations, I sat happily chatting with Janie. The medical professionals in whose hands I was about to put my life still seemed to be out of synch, but I assured myself that this surgery was no big deal—just like my knee operation. I'll never forget the words my wife and I exchanged as I was wheeled down the hall to the operating room:

"I love you, Janie. See you in a little bit."

"I love you more!" she called back.

"No," I said, "I love *you* more!"

Our little game went back and forth all the way down the hall until the operating room doors swung shut behind me. As I was positioned on the surgeon's table, Janie's words were drowned out by the cold voice of the anesthesiologist as he recited the customary "count backwards from 10" cadence. Darkness closed around me before he got to 7.

It was on that table, in that suburban hospital and in that anesthetized state, that I found out what it's like to die—and what it's like to come back from the dead.

Before I Died

Just 10 days before, Janie and I had the best (or one of the best) Thanksgivings in our 25 years of marriage. My physical and emotional powers were firing on all eight cylinders—maybe even nine cylinders. Although the surgery was scheduled, I didn't think much about it. There was turkey and pie to eat.

I don't know what made this Thanksgiving so special. Perhaps it was the perfect mix of people we invited to celebrate the day with us. Our very good friends Rose and Maryann were present for the twentieth straight year. Mother and daughter, Rose and Maryann live together and embody the best of what people can be. When they pray, things happen. When they love, people are moved. We have watched their actions change hundreds of lives. They are a joy to be around.

Also in attendance were Dan and Mary Porter. When Janie and I came to Cincinnati to launch a church in 1985, we had no local contacts. We had no one to turn to and no one to help us get started. Dan was one of the first people I met. He was just 19 and was going to college, trying to figure out what to do with his life. Over the years, I've been a friend to Dan and watched as he launched a graphic arts business, married a wonderful woman and started an amazing family. Janie and I count Dan and Mary as two of our closest friends.

Our oldest daughter, Rebekah, was also at our Thanksgiving dinner, at least for a while. She was 17 at that time and a senior in high school. Rebekah is very outgoing and has a huge social circle, so she was with us for just a few hours before she went off to be with friends. But let me brag a bit about her. When anyone enters a room in which Rebekah is present, she jumps to her feet, engages them, shakes their hand and makes them feel as if they are important. And guess what—she really believes that every person *is* important.

When Rebekah was about 5 years old, I told Janie, "I predict that our daughter will grow up to become a salesperson." Today, Rebekah has a successful pharmaceutical sales career in San Diego, California. She landed a highly sought after job, even though she was 10 years younger than those she was up against for the position.

Laura is our second oldest daughter. She helped cook the Thanksgiving meal. Laura is very different from Rebekah. She is an artist. At this Thanksgiving, she was 14 and in the ninth grade. By nature Laura is on the quiet side, but at about that time in her life she was in the midst of a metamorphosis. She realized, as she wrote in her journal, that what she wanted out of life required her to be an extrovert rather than an introvert.

As a parent, at times it was painful to watch Laura take heartrending steps of change. But by sheer will power, she evolved from one sort of person into a very different sort. With Laura's transformation came more friends and a lot more fun at school. When Laura graduated from high school a few years later, the yearbook profiled the six most intriguing people in the senior class of 1,500 people. Laura the extrovert was one of them.

Our son, Jack, born seven years after Laura, was just 7 years old on that Thanksgiving. He was in the second grade. We had put Jack into school a year early because he tested well and because he was so large physically. He has always been an engaging and likeable kid. On this Thanksgiving, he entertained us.

Jack looks a lot like me. Today, he is a couple of inches taller than I am, even though he is now just 15. He is an amazing guitar player and photographer. I have these skills as well—but to be honest, he is much better at both!

That was our group—my family and some dear friends, the people closest to me in the world. Nothing particular happened on that Thanksgiving, but it was perfect. Toward the end of the day, Janie and I said to one another, "This is one of the best Thanksgivings ever! It won't be like this much longer. Our kids will be going off to college, so let's just soak it in and be thankful." Little did we know how prophetic our passing observation would be.

Janie's birthday was a few days later and my family wanted a night out to celebrate together. The playhouse in town was presenting *A Christmas Carol.* I had previously seen the performance at least three times and didn't feel like going again, but I decided to be a good sport and go along with the party.

As it turned out, I was to receive a message that night. Like Scrooge, I was about to get a scary, life-changing preview of Christmases yet to come. I was about to see ghosts and angels face to face. I was about to look at death head on and find out what it meant to be a cripple like Tiny Tim. I was about to be an unwilling participant in terrifying and soul-challenging events. Most important, I was about to hear God speak to me in ways that would turn my world upside down.

In a matter of just a few hours, the comforting Christmastime drama that unfolded before my eyes that night was to become disturbingly painful and real. Perhaps it was a premonition, but by intermission I was so convinced that I shouldn't go through with the next day's surgery that I asked Janie to call our family doctor and cancel it. She called his number but got his voice mail, so she left him a message asking that he call off the surgery. I wanted to keep my gall bladder. After we got home that night, the doctor called. By the time I got off the phone with him, I had allowed myself to be talked back into it.

Not So Routine

"Six . . . five . . . four"—Janie, of course, did not hear the anesthesiologist's countdown and did not see me fade to black. She had returned to the waiting room and was drinking coffee and chatting with my secretary, Reese. In her mind, everything would be fine.

After what seemed like forever, a hospital staffer finally appeared and told Janie and Reese that my surgery had *just* started. Janie recalls thinking, *That's odd*, but not much more. After 45 more minutes, a nurse ushered Janie and Reese into a small conference room.

"Something's gone awry," the nurse announced in a flat, matter-of-fact tone. "There's been a bit of a problem and Steve won't be going home from the hospital today."

"What happened?" Janie exclaimed.

"Steve's bleeding a lot, and he's going to be sick for a long time. He should be out of surgery and in a room shortly."

It was clear that the nurse didn't want Janie or Reese to panic, but it was too late. Janie wobbled into the women's restroom, where she cried out to God. Her voice echoed off the sterile tiles as she pleaded with all of her heart, "Oh God, Oh God, Oh God, help! Please don't let Steve die!"

The dull beige bathroom walls offered little comfort, so Janie returned to the conference room. She was numb. *Why hadn't Steve used the marker to write out instructions on his abdominal area?*

Reese had already gone into action. She called people—everyone she could think of—and said the same three words to them: "Pray for Steve!"

Nurses and doctors gave Janie and Reese sketchy updates several times each hour. The news didn't get any better as the day wore on. I had lost consciousness and was bleeding a lot. Doctors had been called in to resuscitate me. In a short while, the picture became a bit clearer: My aorta had mistakenly been pierced—not once but twice, front and back. Now there were serious complications.

Word spread quickly. By evening, news of my accident was carried on local radio and television. One leading radio show ran hourly updates on my condition. I even made the six o'clock news. As for me, I was in the process of dying and coming back to life, so I neither heard nor saw any of this.

Some people received a call in the middle of that first night; others didn't hear about what had happened until the next afternoon. Soon, friends began to show up at the hospital. Janie tells me that the news came as a punch in the gut for everyone. *It can't be Steve. I just saw him. He was in fine shape just a few days ago. Close to death? How can that be?* Today, people still speak of where they were when they first heard the news. For me, this is strange to hear. I guess I had more friends than I knew.

That afternoon I was moved into the Intensive Care Unit, where I was hooked up to a ventilator that kept me alive. Janie tells me that I was agitated and uncomfortable with the ventilator tube stuck down my throat. She spent most of the day in shock, trying to make sense of all the medical jargon that the doctors were telling her about my condition. Finally, around midnight, the doctors and nurses convinced Janie that nothing was going to change overnight. So, reluctantly, she went home to get some rest.

In the Middle of the Night

Janie took the phone to bed with her and had just fallen asleep when it rang. It was a nurse from the ICU. "You need to get down here," the nurse said. "They are taking Steve into surgery again."

Janie later told me, "I got the idea that if I wanted to see you alive I'd better get down to the hospital. I felt like the wind had been knocked out of me, and I could barely stand up. As I got dressed I glanced at your closet, and the realization smacked me in the face that you might never come home and wear those clothes again."

Janie was in no shape to operate a car, so she asked Rebekah to drive. Laura also came along. Not wanting to face the crowd of friends gathered in the waiting room, Janie and the girls found an empty room where they could be alone.

Nurses summoned Janie and the girls when I was about to go in for my second surgery. During this roll down the hall, there was no playful banter—I was completely sedated; Janie did all of the talking. Though I could not hear a word, she reminded me of our plans to move to Florida in the future to plant churches among other aging baby-boomers. "Come on, big guy," she prodded. "You can make it. I don't want to go to Florida by myself!"

CHAPTER 2

DYING FOR A MIRACLE

It was a beautiful day to die. I was fading—fast. My vital signs had all but ceased, and the end was just moments away.

Doctors had suspected that I was hemorrhaging internally, so they pumped me full of fresh blood and fluids. Curiously, when the medical team opened me up during my second trip to the operating room, they discovered that I hadn't bled as much as they had initially thought. Instead of reviving me, the added fluids had caused my entire body to swell and my internal organs to suffocate. I ballooned from 180 pounds to 315 pounds in just a few hours. I looked like a cross between the Michelin Man and the Pillsbury Dough Boy!

My Lazarus Story

We don't often get to hear from someone who has died and come back to life. Lazarus was resurrected, but we are never told of his experience while he was out of his mortal body, nor do we learn much about how he lived after he was revived. Death and resurrection, for the most part, remain shrouded in mystery.

Since I'm writing this book, it's obvious that I didn't stay dead. So, I have decided to tell my own Lazarus story. In chapter 1, I painted the bigger picture of my life-and-death struggle. (Yes, I was intentionally dramatic to draw everyone into my story.) Now that we are all tracking, let's backtrack a bit.

Over the course of several months prior to my surgery, I would often experience almost unbearable pain in my midsection, sometimes after eating fatty foods. The attacks were more excruciating than indigestion or heartburn and were followed by numbness and tingling. Because I speak at conferences around the world as part of my job, I travel quite often. I was not interested in suffering such an attack while I was in London or Nashville, so I did the prudent thing and went in for a medical exam.

My family doctor immediately suspected that the problem was with my gall bladder and referred me to a young surgeon, who seemed impressive enough. After all, who am I or any other layman to judge a doctor's credentials? Besides, discovering a doctor's professional successes and failures is about as difficult as breaking into Fort Knox.

I had a sonogram. The results were inconclusive: no visible evidence of a gall bladder, diseased or otherwise. The young surgeon suggested exploratory laparoscopic surgery, in which he would make a series of small incisions in my body that would allow him to explore and, if necessary, remove my gall bladder. In the medical field, this type of surgery has been all the rage. It's popularity stems partly from the shorter post-surgery recovery time for patients. Moreover, a surgeon can perform these non-invasive operations at fast pace.

When the operation was explained to me, it seemed to be rather safe. My surgeon was poised to go and we set the December date. I would be in and out of the hospital in no time flat and back on my feet in time to have Christmas with my family.

A History Lesson

After my accident, I read up on gall bladders—particularly on botched removals. I now know what I should have known before I went under the knife.

About 500,000 Americans have their gall bladders removed each year.[1] Most operations succeed, but some do not. Some victims are quite famous. In February 1975, Aristotle Onassis—one of the wealthiest men on Earth at the time—had his gall bladder removed and died a month later. In 1987, Andy Warhol, the avant-garde artist, went in for the same routine medical procedure, but he died of complications shortly thereafter. A simple search on Google unearths scores of other cases of actual or suspected botched gall bladder removals. Though an exact number is hard to pinpoint, one thing is certain: these botched surgeries do occur!

I find it interesting that both Onassis and Warhol were wealthy men when they died. They probably had the best surgeons that money could hire, and yet they couldn't be saved. The bottom line is that removing a gall bladder is *not* a routine medical procedure.

Since my surgery, I have had literally dozens of people who were facing gall bladder removals come up to me in fear and trembling. I am not a medical professional, but I have learned a thing or two, so I always give the same advice: Be your own aggressive health advocate, do your research, get a second opinion, and go to the largest hospital you can find (I prefer teaching hospitals). No one will look out for you better than you can look out for yourself. But I am getting ahead of myself again.

My Surgery

"Three . . . two . . . one"—the count rapped on, but I was not counting. The surgeon made the first three incisions laterally along my ribcage to create the opening through which he would later insert a piece of surgical equipment. The scars are still clearly visible—each one is just under an inch in length. A fourth incision was made just below my belly button. This opening was to be the space through which the surgeon would insert an instrument so that he could cut a hole and, if necessary, remove my gall bladder.

However, when the surgeon began to make the fourth incision, for some unknown reason he made a tragic mistake. (This was during my first operation, before Janie and my kids knew that anything was wrong.) As I understand it, the surgeon positioned the instrument at an odd angle, something other than the standard protocol of 90 degrees. He then triggered the instrument to fire. However, instead of making a one-inch incision to part my stomach muscles, the cutting device ripped a 3- to 4-inch gash into my midsection. The razor-sharp instrument tore through my intestines, bowel and—worst of all—right through my aorta. It then stuck like a dagger into my spine, severing a number of nerve bundles.[2]

Anyone who has passed ninth-grade biology knows that the aorta takes all of the blood pumped by the heart and transports it to the vital areas of the body. You can imagine what happened to me when my aorta had two holes in it. Blood squirted from it like a fountain. My blood pressure immediately dropped to 50/30 (somewhere around 120/80 is considered normal). One of my doctors described it as having the blood pressure of a sponge.

Although I was bleeding, the surgeon did not realize it. He was surprised and perplexed when my blood pressure began to crash. He saw no sign of bleeding when he looked into the front stomach cavity. Gravity was causing the blood to drain out of my veins and into the hollow of my back.

Words of Assurance

By this time, I was looking up toward the ceiling. I could see light and I could hear a different voice—the voice of God. He was speaking out loud—yes, His words were audible. I knew intuitively that God was the one who was addressing me. It was like the voice of a hundred friends talking in harmonious unison. It was a voice that was familiar and comforting and drew me near. It was safe. Yet at the same time, it was also the earthshaking voice that I imagine Moses must have heard coming from the burning bush in the desert several thousand years ago. God had spoken at a time when Moses desperately needed hope and direction. I am no Moses, but I can now see how much I needed to hear from God at that moment in the hospital operating room in suburban Cincinnati.

In all my years of seeking God, I had never before heard Him speak audibly (nor have I since that time). In fact, I'd never met a person who had heard God talk out loud. This kind of communication is *very* unusual. Maybe it is something that God does only in emergencies. So, when I first heard God's voice, I was alarmed—until I listened to what He had to say.

"Don't be afraid," God assured me. "You have nothing to fear. It's all going to be okay." I wasn't exactly afraid—I was more amazed at what was going on in the room. It was like those movies from the 1970s that show a person on an acid trip.

Slowly floating toward the ceiling, I looked down at the commotion. My view was similar to that of a camera hinged to the bottom of a helium balloon carriage. Suddenly, it occurred to me that what I was seeing below was me. It was strange and dreamlike. I was at peace because God had given me assurance. Up to this time, I had always thought that people who said they heard God's voice were kooks. But there I was, joining the club.

Heart–Stopping Words

The doctor conferred with the anesthesiologist. Suspecting that I was suffering a heart attack, they flipped me over on my stomach. That didn't seem to help. Precious seconds ticked by as they sought to uncover the real problem. Other doctors came running into the room. Eventually, the surgeon made a larger cut into my midsection and discovered the mistake. Another doctor reached carefully down inside my body cavity and held his fingers over the two holes in my aorta.

This Hans Brinker-like approach to stemming the tide of the broken dike stretched on for minutes. My doctor placed an urgent call for dozens of units of B-positive blood (my blood type). *That can't be right,* the nurses thought when they saw the request. They'd never heard of such a large order of blood product. The human body only holds about 17 units.

The doctors could not find the veins in my arms. I have recessive veins—they are rather shy to begin with—and they had collapsed upon themselves due to the lack of blood pressure. After several attempts, the doctors made contact in each arm. The process of pumping blood into me began and the doctors continued to do chest compressions to keep my heart pumping, even though it made the blood that they were pumping into me rush out again.

My blood pressure plummeted even further. My heart struggled to beat. The flow of blood through my arteries and veins stalled, and then almost stopped. After a few minutes my blood pressure dropped even lower, and then lower again. Finally, my heart came to a halt. The line went flat on the screen of the monitor. Alarm buzzers sounded.

"He's coded!" the anesthesiologist yelled. My surgeon cussed. The two called each other names. The nurses scrambled for more help. As I floated out of my body I wavered back and forth, but I could clearly see the surgeon as he freaked out.

My heart was stopped for seven minutes, but it seemed like hours. The Bible declares that God can take time and make it like a rubber band: "A day is like a thousand years, and a thousand years are like a day."[3] As the clock ticked, I heard God speak. He told me about my life and all that He wanted to change in it. It was as if we had taken a trip to the woodshed, in the most positive sense of the expression.

God gave me a number of life-altering, unforgettable messages that I will take to my grave. Some I can share, some are more personal. These words from God have become the center of my life, and I now speak of them constantly.

A Heart-Starting Act

Back in the operating room, someone got on the intercom to call out for more help—"*Stat!*" Doctors and nurses in surgical gowns poured into the room. Each one tried to help. One doctor gave me chest compressions to keep my heart alive while another doctor made sure that I was given oxygen—both at the same time. My body violently rose and fell, up and down. My feet flopped off the operating table.

It appeared that no one on the surgical team knew how to perform the complicated arterial surgery that I needed. The one doctor in the hospital who was capable was about to leave for lunch. He had his hand on the hospital's door handle when he heard the urgent page sounding over the public address system. That page and his response were the first life-saving acts that would turn my story around. At the last minute, the doctor sewed my aorta back together—in both places!

After my heart restarted, my spirit was sucked back into my body. The movement wasn't violent; it was as if I was in the eye of a hurricane. Strangely, I was aware of all that was going on in the operating room, but I was the only one who had heard God's voice.

My heart had stopped and then restarted. I was out of my body and then back in it. Did I die? Was I resurrected? The doctors and I may differ on these points, but one thing I know for certain: God had spoken to little ol' me.

My Struggle to Live

Even though I was knocked out physically, I was aware spiritually. I was wheeled back into the ICU, which, in this instance, was just a glorified room with a couple of adjustments (don't forget, I was in a small suburban hospital).

The nurses went to work on me. They removed my wedding ring in anticipation that my body would swell with the influx of blood product. They placed a ventilator tube down my windpipe. I could vaguely feel the discomfort and wondered what was happening to me.

The leak in my aorta was finally stopped, but by this time the massive blood loss had taken its toll. My body puffed up. My veins were like wet rags, not wanting to hold themselves together.

While people ran around like crazy, I continued my peaceful conversation with God. We did not communicate just with words, but also with memories and images. God let me know how much He valued me. It's almost impossible to describe the perfect sense of acceptance that surrounded me, yet even in the midst of this very personal embrace, part of me knew that not everything in my life had matched what God had intended for me. I had fallen down so often that the angels probably had headaches. Despite my list of fiascos, God extended His total acceptance and absolute love to me—and showed me how He was going to give me another chance.

I got the sense that God was going to give me an opportunity to let go of the things that had become idols in my life and allow me to begin to embrace people instead. I was to become the husband and father that I was supposed to be. Right there in the ICU ward, I realized that I didn't know the names of any of my children's friends! I was to become the employer, neighbor and friend that I was intended to be. I was to become a turtle instead of a rabbit.

A turtle. That is what I would be!

Notes

1. Dave Murray, "Women Exercise and Healthier Gallbladders," *Safety and Health Magazine,* National Safety Council, December 10, 1999. http://www.nsc.org/pubs/sh/gram1299.htm#A (accessed October 17, 2005).

2. These findings regarding the cause of the accident were based upon information provided to me by a number of doctors at the various medical facilities where I was admitted.

3. 2 Peter 3:8, *NIV.*

CHAPTER 3

DANCING AT DEATH'S DOOR

Before I could become a turtle, I needed another miracle.

My doctors have told me that a human body in crisis tries to protect the brain and the heart. Other organs have a lesser priority. After my accident, my colon began to die and my kidneys started to shut down. My torn intestines released toxic gastric fluids throughout my system. A deadly septic infection set in within a day or two because of the toxins that were released. On top of that, it wasn't until four days after the operation that doctors discovered I had developed e-coli from the waste product that was floating through my blood. Both of these infections kill the majority of people who contract them.

Hope was at an all-time low, running on empty.

S-O-S

My daughter Rebekah was remarkable. Like a captain trying to save a sinking ship, she started calling all of her friends and asked them to pray. She reached one friend, Kristen, whose father was a well-known trauma and transplant surgeon at a regional hospital in Cincinnati. Kristen was so shaken by Rebekah's news that she called her father's emergency pager using their special 9-1-1 code. When Kristen's father, Dr. Douglas W. Hanto, called back, she pleaded with him, "You've got to help Rebekah's dad!"

Dr. Hanto immediately went to get the authorization to transfer me to his hospital's far larger and better-equipped facility. The head of surgery already knew about my plight and gave his approval—a member of my men's group had called minutes earlier and told him, "I have a friend who is like a brother to me, and he needs help!" Dr. Hanto volunteered to head the team and be responsible for my care.

Janie calls the people who came to my rescue her white knights. The situation went from absolute panic to great hope when she heard the words "We can help!"

It took five hours to move me from my hospital bed to the ambulance gurney. My vital stats fluctuated at the least bump or jostle. Janie somehow revived at least a measure of confidence. She later told me she knew in her heart that if I just made it alive to the second hospital, I would survive.

It was almost Christmas, but no one seemed to notice. There was no thought about drinking eggnog, opening presents or singing "O Come All Ye Faithful."

New Digs, New Battle

I settled into an exclusive suite at the largest teaching hospital in Cincinnati. The sign on the door read "ICU—Intensive Care Unit." All unauthorized personnel were barred from entering the ICU as Dr. Hanto and his team of medical professionals waged war against death.

My body was suffering and couldn't keep itself alive. The ventilator pushed air in and out of my chest. My hands were tied to the bed in case I awoke and tried to yank out the unnatural hose-like object that was lodged in my mouth and went down my throat. A catheter collected my urine, and mechanical pillows inflated and deflated around my calves to keep blood clots from forming.

The doctors were eager to get a good look around my insides to assess the damage. Part of my liver was dead and had to be removed. Part of my colon and large intestine couldn't take the stress of my low blood pressure and began to disintegrate. This necessitated a colostomy so that waste could be diverted out through the side of my belly. This procedure involves making a hole (which doctors call a "stoma") and attaching a plastic bag to it that is connected to the body through a Tupperware-style seal. If all went well, waste would exit my body through this hole.

During surgery, Dr. Hanto and his team noticed that when my body was cut wide open, my vital signs improved markedly. So they did something unusual: They covered my wound with what seemed to be a layer of medical plastic wrap and left it open, hoping that the massive swelling would subside.

I was placed into a medically-induced coma. My coma was deep enough that I didn't endure the tremendous pain that I would have otherwise experienced due to the swelling and multiple surgeries that took place during the next few weeks. At the previous hospital, I had remained conscious at all times and was in constant pain.

While I was in a coma, some interesting things happened. For one, God continued to speak to me. This time, however, the voice was not audible but internal. It was a voice somewhat similar to the one that I had heard at earlier times in my life, such as when I was in college and went through what I would call a spiritual renewal. In the ensuing years, I have heard from God many times and in many ways. But this was all new. Different. Profound.

At the first hospital, although I was out of it, I had been aware of everything that was going on around me. I had even been aware of talk about pulling the plug on me. Some of the doctors were convinced that I was a goner, yet I could comprehend what they were saying.

At the teaching hospital, even when I was in the induced coma, I could tell when people were speaking positively or negatively about my situation. Some people would come into my room and just weep. Others would ask morbid questions about my mortality chances.

I'm convinced that many people in similar situations are cognizant of what is going on around them when others perceive that they are gone mentally. For that reason, I will never sign a living donor card for myself. I don't want doctors to make life and death decisions about me based on a document that I signed once upon a time when I was healthy. There's no telling what can happen by the power of God in any given medical situation. When He gets involved, *everything* is subject to change. I'd rather take my chances with a long-term stay in the hospital than be prematurely disconnected from life-saving means.

Unusual Visitors

My wildest experience during my dance with death happened about a week into my stay at the second hospital. I was out of the coma but at another critical stage. I was fighting both an e-coli infection and a septic infection in my blood stream, and my condition was complicated further by the fact that I had developed a case of pneumonia. It was the perfect recipe for disaster.

One morning, I woke up from a deep sleep and saw four people surrounding my bed. They were holding hands, and I instantly recognized it as a prayer circle. The people's heads were bowed in reverence; they looked pretty serious. They also looked odd—they were all translucent.

If God had not already spoken to me during my surgery and subsequent hospital stay, I probably would have been frightened at the sight of these people. But by this point I just took in the strange events as they came.

As I gazed at these people, I was intuitively aware of each person's age and knew that they all had succumbed in the ICU during the past few days. I also knew the cause of each person's death. One 19-year-old had died in a car accident. A 30-year-old woman had died in a different wreck. Another man who was present had died after having a stroke—he was in his early 50s. The fourth person, a male in his mid-40s, had succumbed to a heart attack. Later, after my breathing tube was removed, I asked about each of these people. I was correct about each person's age and cause of death. I was also able to correctly identify which bed each person came from in the ICU. (I know, strange stuff.)

As this quartet bowed their heads, I could tell that they were praying for me. I could also tell that they were all followers of Christ (another fact that I later investigated and confirmed to be true). I wondered why they were praying for me. I didn't know it at the time, but I was at a very critical point—probably the most critical since the day of my original surgery when my heart had stopped.

While this group prayed, something powerful happened. My spirit once again started to depart from my body. Similar to my experience in the operating room, I again had the perspective of floating toward the ceiling. No medical personnel came into the room during this time, which was odd because the hospital staff operated around the clock and someone was always checking in on me. However, someone else did enter at that moment.

Authority Over Death

Out of the blue, Larry Kapchinsky, a friend and a fellow-pastor of mine from the Los Angeles area, walked into my ICU ward. Although I was sedated, strapped to my bed and still hooked up to a ventilator, Larry wisely assumed that I could hear and understand what he was saying. He told me that God had told him to come to Cincinnati just to pray for me. Without wasting a moment, he placed one hand on my head and the other hand on my feet and said, "I command death to flee in the name of Jesus. I command life to enter back into this body now."

Larry spoke with authority. He prayed in the same way that Jesus had often prayed—with short prayers that had great authority, even over death. Larry spoke to death as if it was an entity. He spoke to it as if it had a personality. He also spoke to life in the same manner.

After Larry spoke, the floating sensation ended abruptly and I came back into my body. It happened so fast that if I had been in a car, I would have suffered a case of whiplash! The translucent people were gone, and it was just Larry and me in the ICU room.

I was fully aware of all that had transpired. As I opened my eyes and looked at Larry, I felt as if we both understood that we had just experienced a powerful God moment. I believe that if Larry had not flown in from California, I would have been escorted to the other side by those four praying spirits who were already departed. Although I couldn't talk, I think Larry was aware of how grateful I was for his prayer.

Larry stayed for a couple of hours. Later that night, he caught a red-eye flight back to Los Angeles, and the next morning he spoke at his own church.

Whoopi at My Door

During my stay in the ICU, my condition bounced from one state to another depending on the numbers of infections that I was dealing with and the complications that my body was fending off at the moment. I was not in an induced coma at this point, but physically I was still critical. My charts weren't looking good, and everyone on my medical team was concerned.

To make matters worse, I was far from the model patient. Unaware of how grave my situation was, I was fighting the efforts of the doctors and nurses at every step along the way. I was tired of being in the ICU and pleaded with my wife and others to grab each end of the bed and roll me out of the hospital. In addition, although I was given pain meds and sleeping meds, I had not been getting enough real sleep.

One morning at about 2:30 A.M., a stern-looking individual showed up at my doorway. Although she looked every bit the part of an ICU nurse, she stood out in several ways. She wore jeans, an oversized rainbow-colored sweater and leather tennis shoes. Her hair was arranged in short dreadlocks. She looked a lot like folk singer Tracy Chapman. Her attitude was another matter—with her sharp and cutting remarks, she reminded me of Whoopi Goldberg. In short, she was rude.

When this nurse spoke, I listened. "Look, Mr. Sjogren," she stated firmly. "You are not cooperating with the healing process. If you don't start cooperating with the doctors and nurses and what they are trying to do, you aren't going to make it. It's that simple. You have to get on board with your own healing. I want to see an attitude adjustment in you and I need to see it immediately. Do you hear me?"

With that, Nurse Whoopi turned and walked out of my room.

Wow, I thought. *I didn't realize how sick I was. I guess I'd better start being a better patient.* It was a good thought, but, as I already confessed, I was not such a good patient. In the back of my mind, I entertained the idea of complaining to the hospital staff for sending such an in-your-face nurse.

Whoopi at My Door—Again

The following night, Nurse Whoopi came by my room again—at 2:30 A.M., precisely. I was wide awake. She gave me the same talk, word for word. *Okay,* I thought, *I get it already.* (I couldn't respond to her because I still had the ventilator tube down my throat.)

Nurse Whoopi came by my room yet a third night and gave me a third tongue-lashing—again at precisely 2:30 A.M. I didn't know if that was the time she came on duty and I happened to be the first bed on her list to visit or what. Each night she had been dressed in the same attire. Each night she had showed the same sassy attitude. Each night she had scared me.

By this third night, I thought, *I'm definitely going to be a good boy from now on. No more resisting the doctors and nurses. No more going crazy on them when I'm frustrated.* Surprise. My healing process began to improve from that night forward. Not long after, my ventilator was removed. The doctors thought I was making remarkable progress.

Once I was able to talk, one of the first things that I asked about was the Whoopi Goldberg nurse. I described her in great detail: her dreadlocks, what she wore, the time she approached my room each night. The nursing staff was baffled. They told me that there was no African American nurse on night shift duty during that time frame. Further, they said it was strictly against hospital policy to wear jeans on duty. I suggested that maybe she was a volunteer. The nursing staff said that there was no way a volunteer would be allowed in the ICU, especially at night.

It took me a couple of days to put the pieces together, but I finally figured out (with the help of a couple of friends who were interested in my recovery) that this must have been an angel who had visited me. Imagine that, an angel visiting little ol' me. I couldn't believe it. God loved me so much that He sent an actual angel from heaven to deliver a message to me at the precise moment I absolutely needed it.

Why Whoopi?

Since getting out of the hospital, several people have asked why God chose to send me an in-your-face angel. Why didn't I get a happy-go-lucky angel like Clarence in *It's a Wonderful Life*? That angel drank a little too much, was very human and seemed to understand the human struggle. He was almost an uncle figure to George Bailey. Why didn't I get an angel with that sort of persona?

I can only conclude that a more direct approach was needed to get my attention. I am high strung, so I needed a slightly hyper angel who would face me head on. When God sent me Nurse Whoopi in blue jeans, He sent me exactly what I needed.

But I still had to become a turtle.

CHAPTER 4

DYING TO BECOME A TURTLE

A hare one day ridiculed the short legs and slow pace of the turtle, who replied, laughing: "Though you are swift as the wind, I will beat you in a race." The hare, believing that she would easily win such a competition, agreed to run against the turtle and proposed that the fox should choose the course. On the day of the race the two started together.[1]

We all know what happens. The rabbit grabs the early lead while the turtle plods along slowly, steadily and far behind the pace. The rabbit, thinking that she has built up an unbeatable advantage, takes a break in the middle of the race and goes to McDonald's for a Big Mac, fries and a soda. She then literally lays down in the middle of the course and falls asleep. When our friend the rabbit wakes up, she discovers that the turtle has already crossed the finish line.

Aesop, the sixth century B.C. Greek philosopher, concludes in his classic fable about the turtle and the hare that real winners go through life at a slower but steadier pace. Some people call this taking time to smell the roses. As I have mentioned, I was a rabbit—a good and fast one. I was lean, mean and in the lead.

Real Winners

Legendary football coach Vince Lombardi once said, "Winning isn't everything, it's the only thing." The sad truth about my pre-surgery life was that I took Lombardi seriously. I lived on the ragged edge. My typical day was consumed by a desire to get ahead. I would compete with anything that moved—and some things that didn't.

In school, my teachers called me hyperactive. I couldn't sit still for five minutes, let alone hours at a time. Picture a ping-pong ball in a wind tunnel—that was me. Nowadays, doctors diagnose ping-pong people as having attention deficit disorder, or ADD. We have all heard of ADD. Rabbits have ADD, and so did I. In fact, I could have been the poster child for ADD.

As a coach, Vince Lombardi wanted to win every game—and he came pretty close to doing it. Many Americans have followed Lombardi's lead, and an all-consuming appetite for competition has become a positive thing. I was very competitive. As a pastor, I wanted to have one of the largest churches in America. Everything I did went toward reaching that goal. For me, having a successful ministry wasn't everything; it was the only thing.

However, another great American coach, John Wooden, had a very different approach. In *Coach Wooden's Pyramid of Success*, the former UCLA basketball coach (who won 10 national titles) wrote:

Winning seems so important, but it actually is irrelevant. Having attempted to give our all is what matters—and we are the only ones who really know the truth about our own capabilities and performance. . . . The real determining factor is this: Did I make the effort to do my best? That is the only criteria, and I am the only one who knows (well, me and God). Am I a success? I have peace of mind.[2]

What? Winning is irrelevant? I was living as if winning was the only thing that mattered! Success is peace of mind? Peace with God? Wooden may be on to something.

The one who wins in the end is not always the odds-on favorite. In fact, in America we like underdogs. Often in good story telling—such as in Aesop's fable—it's the underdog or the least likely candidate who somehow gets the reward. In the *Lord of the Rings* trilogy, the Hobbits, the little people who were so weak they could barely fend for themselves, save the day. Against all odds, they pull off remarkable victory after impossible victory. They face and conquer the incredible evil forces in Middle Earth. In the end, the ones with the brute strength, the forces of Sauron, are soundly defeated by beings who are less than four feet tall.

When the dust settles, the real winners don't even have to be the ones who cross the finish line first. Look at Jesus. In many ways He wasn't much of a winner—at least not by the world's standards. His own people rejected Him. He had a questionable family background—His mother was pregnant before she married her husband. Apparently, Jesus wasn't much to look at outwardly. He was continually misunderstood, not only by the general public but also by His closest friends. And look at the way He died—alongside criminals, no less.

I could write more about what it means to be a real winner, but I think that I've made my point. Actually, it was God's Word pointed toward me. Before I could slow down, I had to tweak—no, I had to completely change—my view of what it meant to be a winner.

What about having the largest church? Being number one? Succeeding? What about peace of mind?

Slow Down to Catch Up

Being strapped to a hospital bed forced me to immediately change my pace. There was no choice. I had no option. For me, it was the Big Slow Down.

At the hospital, the line of people who came to see me snaked down the hallway. According to the hospital personnel, more people came to see me than had come to see any other patient in the hospital's history.

Maryann, our Thanksgiving guest, visited me at the hospital. She told me that God wasn't through with me—in fact, she insisted that the best was yet to come. Her words were so encouraging that they pumped me up to fight the good fight. They empowered me to press on during that crucial time. Although I was on a ventilator at the time and couldn't respond to Maryann, I later told her that her words were remarkably similar to what God had said to me in the operating room as I hovered between life and death. Maybe God and Maryann are so close that they read the same blogs!

Another friend, Carl, also came to visit me. Carl makes $8 per hour doing odd jobs. It seems that each time I see him he has a different job. He lives a simple life and goes from paycheck to paycheck, but he hears from God in profound ways. He came to my room and told me that even though I was suffering through much pain, God would eventually use this tragedy for my good. Carl said that he saw a picture of a man carrying a backpack that was a heavy burden, but that once the man laid it down he was propelled forward with great force—the backpack had been replaced with a rocket pack!

As I took those words to heart, tears came to my eyes. But other visitors brought in messages that could have brought tears of anger. When people saw me literally tied to the bed in four-point restraints (hands and legs), some viewed this as an opportunity to vent. The word got out: "Hey, Steve is immobile! Let's have at him!" Most of the time, my fear of what these people might say was unfounded. What they actually said to me was much kinder than what I thought they might say.

Then there were the people who took my condition as a chance to light up burning bags of dog doo, ring my doorbell, and run. One person stopped by and announced that this injury was God's wrath upon my life and ministry for my lack of faithfulness to God's Word. He said that I was a sinner and that God was judging me. He came on like an Old Testament prophet. All he was lacking was a robe and a staff.

God's message was loud and clear: He wanted me to decelerate and walk in a more balanced way of life. His words were strong. He said that my life had been a lie. Publicly, I had the appearance of living in balance, but privately—when all of the trappings were stripped away—I was anything but balanced. In the weekly messages that I gave at church, I talked about how to live a balanced life. I had lots of practical pointers and told great stories. I was good at teaching others how to do it. The problem was that I wasn't doing it myself.

Sometimes God can be downright sneaky in the way He drives home a point. To be sure that I got the word on slowing down, He sent messengers to me. From these messengers, I learned a valuable lesson that I had been avoiding like the plague—that when we slow down, certain people whom we may have been avoiding catch up with us. The crazy thing is that to have any hope of achieving balance in our lives, we really need to hear from both parties—those whom we want to see and those whom we may have been avoiding.

In my life, I needed to hear both from people who thought that I was great and from people who didn't like me at all. I needed to hear from people whom I had conflict with and those whom I did not. I needed to hear from people who loved my vision and those who couldn't relate to my leadership—mostly because they were opposed to change, which I was bringing all of the time.

A Surprise Visit

I was surprised to see one particular visitor. He had been hired as my assistant on staff at our church a year before, but things just hadn't worked out. He was skilled, multi-talented, fun to be around and very intelligent. Unfortunately, he wasn't the right guy for that job. I had to fire him, and I agonized over his departure for weeks. Before the accident occurred, we had been avoiding one another. He was the last person I expected to see at the hospital when I was down.

When he entered my room, it was awkward. I wasn't sure what to say or how to react. After all the pain he had gone through, I assumed that he would be bitter. Instead, I found out that on the day I was moved from the first hospital to the larger teaching hospital, he had risked getting a big speeding ticket by driving 85 miles per hour just to keep up with the ambulance! As it turned out, next to Janie, throughout my recovery he was the most attentive person around.

Some time later I asked him, "Why did you stick by me after all that I put you through? You lost your job. You moved across the country to take this post and it didn't work out. You have every reason to be bitter or at least upset, but you took the high road and became a servant to me. What gives?"

What he said was one of the greatest lessons on grace that I will ever learn. "I felt called by God to come out here to be your assistant," he replied. "That call came from God, not from you or any other person. Jesus called me to this task. I don't think that you ever needed an assistant more than you needed one when you were in the hospital. I wasn't about to drop you when you needed me the most. Sure, I was hurt. Sure, it was a challenge to continue to support you. But I pushed forward by the desire that God gave me in my heart."

This man and I have gone on to become close friends. I've even cowritten a book with him.

The Scary Hospital

Once my recovery was underway, I was moved to a third hospital. It was at this facility that my physical rehabilitation began, after the initial crises were over.

To me, this third hospital was a scary place. People with simple sports injuries were treated next to severely brain-damaged patients. I wasn't sure where I fit—and I didn't want to stay long enough to find out. I was in a state of continual watchfulness. I felt that I was seriously in danger for my life. Every week I saw patients die. These patients were close by, and it seemed as if they were all around me.

Being at that hospital reminded me of working at an underground copper mine one summer while I was in college. My job was to carry dynamite. All summer long men died all around me. In fact, two men died on the shift right before me doing the exact same job that I was doing. I was paid very well—$25 per hour in 1976, which was enough to pay for all of my expensive private college bills that year and then some—but the possibility of death was always at hand.

Friends, people from my church and even people whom I didn't know stopped by to see me and volunteer to help. I always took them up on the offer. I asked them to wash my hair, shave my face or clean my ears—all of which were humbling, but made me feel much better afterwards.

A friend of mine named Doug visited me at the scary hospital. Doug lived in Seattle, but he was in the region to speak at a college. He had been following my situation and somehow tracked me down. When Doug popped his head into my room, the atmosphere immediately changed. In that moment, everything was not so scary.

My theory is that God gives some people the actual gift of laughter. Doug has that gift. Wherever he goes, people who meet him enjoy themselves and find themselves at ease. It wasn't long before Doug and I were laughing at the top of our voices.

Doug is also a great storyteller. He told me about the time that he was showing a group of businessmen around the site on which he wanted to build a church. He was trying to act spiritual, so he stopped to pray for the property. Unfortunately, he stopped in the wrong place—right in the middle of some quicksand. It only took a few moments for him to sink up to his armpits. The businessmen had to form a human chain to save his life. They all ruined their expensive suits and lost their Gucci loafers. Doug was left with nothing but his boxers! It was tragic, but it couldn't have happened to a funnier guy than Doug. We were laughing so loud that the nurses stopped by twice and asked us to shush. Doug's two-hour visit lifted my spirits for a good week.

The next night, another friend, John, caught up with me. John is a pastor from Madras, India, who starts churches all over south central India. The summer before my injury, John and his wife, Carol, had come to visit Janie and me in Cincinnati. He couldn't believe that I was now in such horrible condition. After all, I had been in such great shape just a few months before. John isn't funny like Doug, but he has a great bedside manner and is a natural encourager. When I asked John what he was doing in the United States, his answer shocked me: He said that he had come halfway around the world just to see me!

John and I talked for several hours that evening. The next morning, John came back and accompanied me to my physical therapy. We had a great time laughing and smiling through the painful experience of trying to get my legs to work.

When John left later that day, I felt that I was lifted greatly and that I had been encouraged beyond what words could express.

A Thank-fest and Humble Pie

When we slow down, people will catch up with us. I had to go to the hospital and almost die—twice—to learn the value of this. I still have to remind myself to slow down and be a turtle. But I am getting better at it. I'm also getting far fewer bags of burning dog doo left on my doorstep.

The Bible says that when we have offended someone or when someone has accused us of doing something wrong, we should go quickly to that person. Jesus was pretty clear about it. He said, "When someone has something against you, go to that person and make it right."[3] I was running scared, thinking that a long parade of people were angry with me for something that I had done or said over the years. Of course, I wasn't really sure of what all I had said or done (or not said or not done). How could I know? I was running so fast that I had probably offended myself and not even noticed.

I feared that slowing down would open the gates for people to react to me. But once I allowed people to catch up with me, their responses were overwhelmingly positive. They were genuinely grateful and thankful for what I had done for them. As I look back, I realize that I had irrational fears. I thought that people would line up to tell me off, but all they wanted to do was to serve me and thank me. It was a thank-fest, and rather humbling.

Aesop wrote a fable about a boy, who reminds me of myself. This boy was in a hurry to get a snack. As the fable goes:

> A boy put his hand into a pitcher full of hazelnuts. He grasped as many as he could possibly hold, but when he tried to pull out his hand, he could not remove it, for the neck of the pitcher was too narrow. The boy desperately wanted his hazelnuts, but he was unable to get them and he burst into tears. A visitor saw the boy's pain. Instead of taking the chance to further sully the young lad, the visitor [probably a classmate the young boy had been avoiding] made a kind suggestion. "Be satisfied with half the amount," he said, "and you will easily draw out your hand."[4]

All right, already, Aesop. I get the message!

Notes
1. Aesop, *The Turtle and the Hare*, a loose adaptation. Public domain.
2. John Wooden, *Coach Wooden's Pyramid of Success* (Ventura, CA: Regal Books, 2005), pp. 134-135.
3. See Matthew 5:24.
4. Aesop, *The Boy and the Hazelnuts*, a loose adaptation. Public domain.

CHAPTER 5

DYING TO BE NORMAL

I am not a big baseball fan, but I do know who Barry Bonds is. Bonds is just the third player in major league history to eclipse the 700-career-home-run mark and, barring serious injury, he should make a good run at Hank Aaron's all-time best of 755.

Bonds—no doubt a rabbit—had a huge setback in 2005. A set of injuries kept him in the dugout for most of the season. As the final weeks of the season approached, Bonds's teammates, the San Francisco Giants, were still in contention for a pennant. Bonds could not resist the urge to get back to where the action was, and because of this he probably rushed his return to the lineup. But who can blame him? I can't. I know the feeling.

Seven weeks and three hospitals after my accident, I went home. It was strange and wonderful at the same time. Janie was relieved—I would again wear those clothes hanging in the closet—and she helped me get started on a regimen of home-based therapy.

After a couple of months, I felt that I needed to be back in action—back to speaking in public. I decided to make Easter morning the day of my return.

In the Gardens

At that time, our church, the Vineyard Community Church in Cincinnati, was meeting in a facility that was designed to hold just 550 people. To accommodate the weekend attendance that regularly eclipsed the 4,000 mark, the church held seven different services. For my return, the staff and I decided to rent one of the largest venues in the city, the 25,000-square-foot Cincinnati Gardens, which has hosted rodeos, monster truck jams, professional hockey games and presidential campaign rallies. Elvis Presley, Madonna and the Grateful Dead have all played there. But on Easter 1998, it was ours.

I rode in to the Gardens with John Edgar, one of the most energetic and positive people I know. We had allowed enough time, but there was a traffic jam. *Great,* I thought. *The one day that we hold services downtown we get stuck on the highway with a million other cars. What else will go wrong?* As we edged closer, I realized that all of the cars were headed toward the Gardens. I was humbled. (This humility thing would become a recurring theme, but I was still uncomfortable with it.)

John parked the car as close as he could to the arena and we made our way inside. In the moments before the service began, I looked around. The place was electrified. You could cut the energy with a knife. To say that people were excited doesn't do the scene justice. The venue was nearly filled—8,000 people had come, twice the number of our regular Sunday attendance!

Most of the program was filled with worship music, prayer and other people speaking. I was to give a short greeting toward the end the service. I am not sure what I was expecting, but it was certainly not what I got. I was so weak that I had to lean heavily on my cane. Without it, I would have fallen on my back in an instant. As I approached the podium, people gave me a standing ovation that lasted for more than two minutes. I was completely taken aback. I had come a long way, but I didn't realize how much I was loved.

After the Easter service, a writer for the Cincinnati Enquirer approached me. "I just sat through the service," he said. "Wow! That was amazing! I was supposed to ask you questions for a front-page article on how the Vineyard filled the Gardens on Easter, but I can't think of any questions. I'm overcome. I just want to say thanks for coming to Cincinnati to start this thing."

I can't take any credit. When that sort of amazing sense of God's presence occurs, who can do anything but stand back and say, "Go, God!"

My Wheelchair Video

Before my Gardens appearance (not at all to be confused with or even slightly juxtaposed with Jesus' ultimate Garden appearance), I needed a wheelchair. I also needed to have some contact with people. My staff and I decided that I would return to our church, and we soon began to make the plans (this was a couple of weeks before the big Easter shindig). However, I knew that I did not have the energy to speak at the services. So how could we pull it off?

A video—that was it! We would make a tape of me getting around in my wheelchair. But the video had to be humorous. I had to poke fun at myself. Thus, the now-famous *Wheelchair Video* was conceived. We played it at every service that first weekend I came back.

Here is how the video went. As the opening scene fades in from black, the assistant pastor, Dave Workman, runs out the side door of the church building. "I've got to find Steve, I've got to find Steve," he says. "Maybe he's at home."

The video cuts to the next scene. The assistant pastor runs into my front yard, up to my door and walks into my house. He calls out my name. I'm downstairs watching a movie.

"What are you doing?" he says.

"I'm just watching *It's a Wonderful Life* for the eighty-seventh time," I say, nonchalantly. "Look at this part. It's my favorite!" Mr. Potter and George Bailey are on the screen. Potter says, "Why, you're worth more dead than you are alive!" (I love that line.)

The assistant pastor isn't amused. "We've got to get you down to the Vineyard," he says. "It's your first week back at church and it's time for you to speak."

In the next scene, the two of us are now upstairs in my home. I'm in my wheelchair. "You might need this for the ride," the assistant pastor says, handing me a full-coverage motorcycle helmet with a tinted visor.

Next we're out in the driveway. "I thought that we'd give you a special drive down to the church to break up the boring physical therapy that you've been going through lately," the assistant pastor says.

"Let's go for it!" I say, always up for a ride.

For the next scene, the video crew switched me out for a dummy dressed exactly like me and wearing the same helmet. First the dummy is in the wheelchair holding on to a rope that is attached to the back of a truck. "Let's go fast!" I say in my voiceover. The driver squeals the tires and the dummy flies out of the chair and bounces on the ground, still holding on to the rope. (When we played the video at the first service, the people in the audience didn't know if they should laugh or not. The scene is hilarious, but uncomfortable.)

"Let's go fast," I say in another voiceover. "*Real* fast. Put some pepper into it!" The driver in the video misunderstands me and puts the truck into reverse. The truck backs into the dummy and the wheelchair, and everything goes flying every which way. (Again, the people watching the video didn't know if they should laugh or not. A few giggled. I loved it. One of my basic credos in life has always been to be the first one laughing at myself.)

The next scene depicts the assistant pastor wheeling the dummy onto a walking bridge that is suspended about 30 feet over a small creek. "How about a bungee jump?" he says. He links together several small bungee cords with hooks on them (the kind used to strap suitcases to the tops of SUVs) and attaches them to the wheelchair. Time to jump! He eases the whole contraption—dummy and all—over the side of the bridge. Of course, as soon as he lets go of the wheelchair, the bungee grips come loose and the wheelchair plummets toward the creek bed at full force. Ouch. After the bridge scene, the song "I Get Knocked Down, but I Get Up Again" plays as brief clips of all the scenes are shown on the screen.

The bridge scene was side-splitting physical comedy. By now, most people in the audience realized that the whole thing was a big gag and that I was making fun of my serious condition. They gave themselves permission to laugh. (I did want to be sensitive to other wheelchair-bound people in our congregation, so I cleared the concept of the video with them in advance.)

When the video credits had rolled and the lights in the sanctuary were back on, the assistant pastor suddenly came running in from the side door, pushing me in the wheelchair. Everybody stood up and cheered and whistled. Some stomped their feet. Others lit up their Bic lighters. It was a madhouse. It was strange. I was humbled.

Now when I watch that video, I don't know whether to laugh or cry. For me, creating it was a way of venting my frustrations with all that had happened. Now it brings back raw emotions. I was glad to be back at the church, but I was still not sure if everyone understood what I had gone through to be there. I wasn't looking for approval from the members of my church or to be some type of hero; rather, I desperately needed to draw strength from them. Indeed, it felt awfully good to be welcomed back with so much enthusiasm.

My New Normal

A funny thing happened that first weekend I came back. As I began to say a few words, I forgot to watch where my wheelchair was going. Suddenly, the front wheels went off the stage and hung in midair. I quickly applied the brakes to avoid a crash, but it was close.

I was absolutely exhilarated about being back after such a long absence and went to as many of the weekend services as I could. Afterwards, I was wiped out. It took me weeks to get rested up—that's how fragile I was. In hindsight, I realize that I returned to speaking much too early.

Like I said, I know how Barry Bonds felt. I wanted so much to get back to normal. I wanted everything to be okay, just like old times. But the reality was that I couldn't do things the way that I had done them in the past. Before my accident, I was always at the gym. I could do several hundred sit-ups a day—seriously. I was in the best shape of my life. Sometimes I would leap onto the stage at church; other times I would jump over four steps. Now I was crippled. I had to get onto the stage by scooting on my knuckles and my rear end, inch by inch.

As much as I wanted to be normal, the reality of my situation was hard to ignore. I could only work for a few hours each week—30 hours was the absolute maximum. That was fewer than half as many hours as I had been putting in during my rabbit days.

I repeatedly asked my doctors and therapists if I was ever going to be healthy again. The answer was always the same. They would look down and pause, and then meekly mumble something about how difficult it was to predict the future. The fact was that they didn't know how much I could recover. They knew that it would be months before I would be able to walk—even with the use of walkers and canes—but they did not know if I would ever walk normally again. At the minimum, they knew that I would always have a residue of a limp. They also had no way of predicting how much numbness I would face throughout my life. All of this was devastating to hear, even when it was accompanied by apologies from the doctors.

One thing was certain: My life would never be the same. This would be my new normal.

The Fear of Not Enough

Before the accident, our family always had enough. Although we were not rich and there were times when we could not buy the latest gadget, we always had shelter, food and clothes. We were never in the red. But with my physical problems came immediate financial pressures.

When I got home, letters awaited me from the suburban hospital where the accident had occurred. Terse words screamed off the page. The billing department was threatening to contact a collection agency for the lack of payment on my three-day stay. That bill and warning turned out to be wrong, but it shocked me into reality. Suddenly, I realized that I could be facing huge medical bills that might jeopardize the financial security of my family.

I had never been one who was afraid of the future. I had consistently taught and counseled people that the future was something they should run toward and never fear. But now I faced a scary unknown.

I had never paid myself well. The priorities of the church were about reaching the community and caring for the needy, so everyone on staff was underpaid. I augmented my salary by frequently speaking at conferences and seminars. Now, the income from my speaking had been cut off (at least temporarily), and my bills were mounting faster than my blood pressure was rising. I feared that I would go into the red for the first time in my married life.

To add to our family's angst, there was a group in the church who felt that I was no longer of any use. They saw me as worn out and needing to be replaced. I was like a totaled car that needed to be traded in for a newer model. These people complained about me—loudly and frequently.

When Fear Comes

Janie and I had to face head on our fear of not having enough. We all battle with this fear in one form or another. We worry that we don't have enough *money, time, friends, love* or *opportunities*, to name just a few. In my travels and interactions with people of various cultures and nationalities, these seem to be universal fears that we all face, no matter how mature we are spiritually or emotionally.

My purpose here is not to give a long or deep explanation, but track with me for a few paragraphs as I describe what Janie and I found to work regarding our finances. As I mentioned, there were people in the church who felt I should be replaced. Fortunately, most of the church leaders saw the situation differently. They actually raised my salary to meet the financial needs of our family and even helped to pay off some of our bills. However, this did not occur until I opened myself up to ask for help, which was something that I wasn't accustomed to doing.

Jesus said, "You have not because you ask not!"[1] I first needed to ask God to provide for our family from His supply. His supply is different than mere human provision. We may fear not having enough, but in God's economy there is always plenty. We think in terms of barely squeaking by—barely meeting the quota. But God provides in absolute abundance. Simply put, He will give us more than we need. He is amazing.

Janie and I strongly believed that the only way to face our fear about not having enough money was to give away a chunk of our funds. We had always operated that way and continued to do so even after my accident, when our funds were depleted. We gave away what seemed to be a significant amount. This jump-started our faith, and then God did the rest. In addition to the help from the church, I was able to earn money from a few speaking engagements, and publishers soon began to accept my book manuscripts.

I believe that these are the keys to facing our fears. We need to give away a significant portion of what we have—specifically that of which we don't think we have enough. For example, if you don't think you have enough time, volunteer what little time you do have. I recommend serving the poor—find a good nonprofit organization and begin to serve on a regular (hopefully, weekly) basis. If you fear not having enough money, give some away. Find a widow, orphan, single mom or homeless person who needs help. The willingness to give away the little that we have demonstrates the faith that God requires of us and paves the way for Him to get involved in our personal situations in a big way. This is God's economics.

God often uses other people to meet our needs, which works in tandem with the desire to help others that He has placed in each of us. It can be humbling when we let our needs be known, but people generally come through. That's my experience. I have found that people really want to help a person in authentic need. People have a heart to help their fellow man. The answer to fear is to step out in faith. This is an old principle, but it is a core part of what would become my new normal.

Adventure in the Dumps

In the midst of my recovery, when I was becoming a bit more mobile, I got an idea. It seemed that everywhere I turned there was a story in a magazine, on a TV show or on a radio program about people in Mexico City who survived by digging through the trash piles. I felt a strong sense that I should go and care for some of those people.

One day, I called an adventurous friend and explained my idea. He told me to count him in. We immediately set a date for the trip, just a few weeks from that time. We both brought a friend.

None of us spoke Spanish. We didn't have any contacts in Mexico City, nor did we know how to get to the dumps. However, about a week before the trip, I received an e-mail from a person whom I had never met. The message was short but said plenty: "If you ever go to Mexico City, you might want to connect with ——." He provided the name of a person who spoke fluent Spanish and who had lived in Mexico City for several years. *Follow the trail of bread crumbs*, I thought. I contacted the person in Mexico City and explained our project. I asked him if he would be willing to show us around and take us to the city dumps. He said that he had always wanted to go to the dumps but was fearful of going there alone.

I have always had a penchant toward action and a disdain for theoretical approaches to life. "Ready, fire, aim!" was my *modus operandi*. Some might call it blind faith, but I find that when I set myself up so that God must show up and provide for me, He typically does. I am not suggesting that it is okay to be irresponsible; rather, I'm just saying that we need to be willing to take risks. Sometimes this means traveling thousands of miles without a clear itinerary or knowing the native language.

Let me give another example of this. When I was fresh out of college, our family (which at the time consisted of Janie and our five-month old baby, Rebekah) moved from the Midwest to Los Angeles to pursue an opportunity at a large church near UCLA. We were about to take a 2,000-mile trip, and all that we had to get there was an old Volkswagen van that constantly needed repairs. That's enough to make anyone a little crazy. Janie was nervous, but I thought it was an adventure. I was so right—and naïve! Fortunately, God can work with naïve.

Just as we were leaving town, a nice couple that we knew drove up to us and handed us an envelope. They said that what was inside would "serve as a gift into our lives." We thought that was interesting, but we didn't quite understand what they were talking about. We didn't even comprehend that they were giving us money. There was close to $1,000 in the envelope! Janie and I were blown away. We had never seen that much money. I had been working three jobs just to keep body and soul together. We pulled out of town with big smiles on our faces.

All that we owned on Earth was jammed into that white hippie mobile. We drove several hundred miles that first day without much incident. On the second day, however, the engine struggled and a cooling tube blew apart. I'm not much of a mechanic, but I knew that what I saw spilling out all over the engine area was cooling fluid. I figured out which tube had come apart, pieced it back together, and then poured in fresh cooling fluid. To my amazement, the engine seemed to work just fine! We continued down the road, saying many prayers and with a fair bit of apprehension.

That night we traveled through the mountains of Arizona, where it was snowing like crazy. Something in our transmission snapped, and we were stranded on the side of the road. The three of us trying to hitchhike at midnight was a comical sight—I was standing by the side of the road holding a small pathetic sign that simply read "HELP!" Finally, we made it to safety and found someone who could check our vehicle. The problem was rather simple to fix, but the repair required a particular part that had to be shipped from Phoenix, which was several hundred miles away to the south.

We had to halt our trip for a few days and bide our time in a small town until the part arrived. By this time, Janie had had it with our van. She asked me—no, she *told* me—that we were going to get rid of that vehicle as soon as we were settled in Los Angeles. She liked to pray, but having to pray each time she got into the van just so that she could arrive in one piece was getting a little ridiculous!

By the time we reached Southern California, we had spent nearly all of the money that the couple had given to us. We had less than $100 left. As I said, we were young and naïve. But God had provided.

All of this is to say that many years later, I went to Mexico with the same "ready, fire, aim!" mentality, although this time we had enough money and the contact that God had provided. What an adventure! The people at the dumps were amazing. Taking such a risk to help people was an impromptu but important step for me to get to my new normal. It was the old me, just in a wheelchair. Maybe the biggest success of the trip was that I didn't get sick! (I always get sick when no one else does.)

In hindsight, I wonder if I would have the guts to do the same thing again. No contacts, no language skills, just a conviction that we were supposed to go to the dumps outside Mexico City.

Note
1. See James 4:2.

CHAPTER 6

DYING TO LET GO

Today is a splendid autumn day. It's unusually warm outside—81 degrees, perfect for a Labor Day picnic. Warbling birds perch themselves on tree limbs and children eat watermelon in downtown Cincinnati's Eden Park. It's a great place for family fun. Hey, the drinking fountains even work at this park, which is a good sign in my book.

Later tonight the picnickers—old and young alike—will ooh and ahh as fireworks light up the riverfront over nearby Sawyer Point. It's hard to believe that some 800 miles to the south another great American city is drowning. Yet when I turn on my plasma TV, I see unbelievable scene after heart-wrenching scene of New Orleans under water. The catastrophic results of Hurricane Katrina break the festive mood of Labor Day just as the warbler's harsh, discordant chirp contradicts the magnificent flight of a red tail hawk over the Ohio River. I would not know the difference between a black-throated green warbler and a Tennessee warbler, but I know anguished people when I see them. And looking into the televised eyes of the men, women and children trapped in the Big Easy, I see pain. I can almost feel it.

Over the years, I have come alongside many people who have faced a sudden personal tragedy or experienced severe grief. I have heard the stories of victims of rape and men who have lost their six-figure-salary jobs. I have listened to stories from the parents of a child who was killed by a drunk driver and from the sister of a girl who committed suicide. The list of grievers is long, and even the expected loss of an elderly parent or a pet can bring it on. I have listened, prayed and held people's hands, usually not knowing what to say.

Whenever a loss cuts someone down, I try to help that person regain a grip on reality. Almost always, the grief-tattered person has to walk through specific stages of recovery. Although I have had disappointments in life, until my accident I never really had to travel this road myself. The day I died, the warblers sang. I am sure of it.

Old Steve, New Steve

When God told me that "it's all going to be okay," I thought He meant that I was just going to survive that day's surgery. Later, I discovered He meant that I would survive the entire physical ordeal. Later still, I came to understand He meant that I would survive and even thrive in an environment of change. How was I going to not only survive but also thrive? Didn't God know that I had a 20-inch slice in my belly that needed to heal and that I would not be able to walk again without the aid of a cane?

I went from thinking, *Wow, I'm going to live!* to *How am I going to live now?* Even though God had spoken and *said* that everything was going to be okay, I had a long way to go before I *reached* okay. I had heard the words but still not fully grasped how deep God would go. It was tough.

Again, I am getting ahead of myself. Before we get to the steps of my recovery, let's revisit my hospital stay for just a moment. One of the first signs as to just how tough my new reality would be came when I was still in the second hospital. After two weeks in ICU, my body was stable enough that I could be moved into a private room. It was in that room on Christmas Eve that I learned more bad news.

An orderly who was in the room to take my vitals slid me to the edge of the bed and began to help me stand on a scale. As he did so, my thigh muscles failed and I slipped like a noodle to the floor. Doctors examined me and concluded that the nerves in my legs had been severely damaged. I needed physical therapy. On New Year's Day, I was moved to the third hospital—the scary one. After three weeks of learning how to use a wheelchair and then a walker, I was released to continue therapy and healing at home. In a way, that is when the real healing began.

The Steps of Grieving

It was many months before I woke up and accepted my reality—my new normal. Along the way, I went through several predictable stages. As I mentioned, people who have experienced grief must walk through several stages of recovery. In her book *On Death and Dying*, the noted psychologist Dr. Elisabeth Kubler-Ross identifies these stages as denial, anger, bargaining, depression and, finally, acceptance.[1]

I was familiar with Kubler-Ross's steps of grieving, but I never pictured myself going through them. Although she applied these steps to the death and dying process, they also fit my loss process. In fact, some counselors point out that Kubler-Ross's prototype was originally created with the idea of anyone going through a catastrophic change in mind. Over the course of the first year of my recovery and rehabilitation, I went through each of these stages step by step.

Step One: Denial

At first, I refused to believe that anything in my situation had changed. *This was just like my knee surgery,* I said to myself. *After a little while, everything will return to normal.* Denial was not only in my head—I actually acted upon it as well. Before my accident, I owned two motorcycles. I love motorcycles. I love the sense of freedom that I get when I'm on a big bike with the wind in my face and the engine thundering beneath me. There's nothing like it!

After my accident, with even a little bit of weight tilted toward my legs, the bike would end up on the ground. I no longer trusted my sense of balance well enough to keep a decent bike up on two wheels. Dr. Hanto, my main life-saving surgeon, warned me: "Don't get back into riding bikes after all that you have been through!" (He actually refers to motorcycles as "donor cycles" because of all the people with head injuries that come in to his care and end up donating their organs after their deaths.) I was too weak to ride, and I had to give both of my motorcycles away. It was a tough move, but a smart one.

I was eventually fitted for leg braces, which made both legs a bit more stable. Not long after acquiring the braces, I got a little crazy. I decided that I wanted to test drive the BMW motorcycle of my dreams. I made my way to a local dealership and ogled the $17,000 machine. Standing there with my leg braces on, I must have looked pretty scary. Although I could barely walk, somehow I talked the salesman into letting me take the bike for a spin. "I'll be back in a bit," I nonchalantly promised.

About 60 seconds after I pulled out of the dealership and onto the road, I realized that I had made a big mistake. I came to a traffic signal. It was red a light, which meant that I had to stop the bike. I tried to lower my legs and anchor them on the pavement to steady the motorcycle. Uh oh—I could barely keep the costly contraption vertical. The thought of dropping the bike scared me quite a bit. If it fell, I didn't know how I would get it back up.

How could I get the bike back to the dealership in one piece? I quickly sorted through my options. I realized that I would be okay if I could avoid coming to a complete stop, so I drove slowly and made a series of long right-hand turns. It took quite a while, but I finally maneuvered my way back to the dealership. By this time, the salesman was beginning to wonder if I had made off with the bike.

I was shaking as I returned the keys. I told the salesman that I wasn't ready to buy the bike and that I had to think about it. In truth, there was no thinking to do—I had learned my lesson. Looking back on the experience, I now realize that I wasn't just dreaming—I was living outside the bounds of what was earthly possible. Motorcycles aren't in my future. That's fine with Janie, and my life insurance rate is lower.

I had other areas of denial as well. I was fixated on this idea of getting back to normal, but my body wasn't cooperating.

Step Two: Anger

My healing progress was slow and the outcome was uncertain. I became angry—angry at God, angry at myself, angry at my situation. Just plain angry.

I tend to hit the anger button faster than most people. My natural tendency is to be passionate about anything, and when you added to this my circumstances after the accident, the result was not pretty. Just about anyone would show some rage at the prospect of losing a great deal of his or her physical abilities. Anyone would be upset at having his or her life turned upside down. Perturbed is another good word.

I was frustrated that I couldn't do what I used to do. I had a bad case of the "shoulds" controlling me. I *should* be able to jump up to the top of the steps. I *should* be able to work 100 hours a week. I *should* be able to attend several two-hour meetings each day—without a break! I *should* be able to speak at all seven of our church's weekend services. I *should* be able to stay up late on Sunday evening after a full weekend of services and write 60 or 70 newcomer letters by hand. I *should* be able to make a couple dozen calls on the phone each day. I felt that I should be able to all of these things. But the simple reality was that after my accident, I *couldn't* do any of them.

I didn't want to be a burden to others, and I didn't want them to pity me. But the reality was that I had to let go of the shoulds to reach the point where I had a realistic view of myself. I came up with a motto for my life at that point: "Don't should on me." Because of the nature of the cause of my injury—that it occurred as a result of a hospital's mistake—I had people coming to me who encouraged me to live in a state of anger and bitterness. They didn't realize what they were doing to me. They thought that they were giving me emotional support, but in truth they were dragging me down. They fed the temptation already present in my mind to spend time blaming others for my situation (and being angry at them) instead of accepting my new reality and moving on. It's ironic how sometimes people can try to help but end up getting in the way. They end up sounding like warblers.

Step Three: Bargaining

Once I got past pointing fingers at the doctors, I started to bargain with God. I wanted to make a deal. Let's eavesdrop on some of my prayers at that time:

> *God, if You just get me back to where I was before all of this happened, I'll change.*

*Heavenly Father who I will faithfully serve all of the days of my
life, if You just restore me physically, relationally and emotionally, I'll take back all of the bad things I've said about others and
I will go to all of the people I've wronged to ask for forgiveness.*

*Jesus, my friend, my buddy, I need Your help. I will be a better hus-
band, a better father and a better pastor if You just give me back
my legs and my motorcycles (okay, just one motorcycle will do).
Amen!*

I sure hope God was smiling as I prattled along. I had confused
the concept of faith with the idea of reality—and I was the pastor
of one of Cincinnati's largest churches!

I didn't stop with misplaced prayers. Somehow, I had come
to think that if I trusted God enough, I would get better no matter what the doctors said. When the doctors gave discouraging
reports about my legs or my neurological condition, I disregard-
ed their statements and turned to God all the more.

There's nothing wrong with trusting God—in fact, we must.
However, by ignoring what the doctors were saying, I was ignoring reality. I was so eager to hear good news that I manufactured
my own. I was basically telling God that if I expressed enough
faith, He had to keep His end of the bargain and heal me. I even
tried some of the formulas of big-name faith healers. I was trying to make any deal that I could with God.

In my eagerness to see healing come my way, I tried to
manipulate God. I "declared" my healing—in other words, I took
a couple of verses on healing out of the Bible, repeated them,
and then told God that I expected Him to heal me right then and
there. I took my cane—the cane that I couldn't walk without—
and tossed it out of the window of my car as I drove down the
freeway! (If you were in the white Nissan Maxima behind me,
I apologize for the flying cane.)

Of course, nothing happened to me physically, because that isn't the way that God works. In my heart I knew that already, but I was desperate to see something happen. When you are desperate, you begin to do odd things. You even deny the reality that you know to be true.

In the end, I realized that this approach was neither reality nor an act of faith. Slowly, I returned to God's Word and began to see the balance the Bible teachers present when it comes to physical healing. We should always pray for the sick—indeed, God does heal people. But we should never try to bargain with God, for He is ultimately sovereign.

Step Four: Depression

When bargaining with God didn't work, I became depressed. I often woke up feeling scared. There weren't a lot of people encouraging me at that point. The crisis was over, so fewer people called or visited. I dropped off of the radar screens of many of my friends. Most people stopped praying for me because it was apparent that I was not going to die. Yet though I wasn't going to die physically, I sure was dying emotionally. This was the most difficult part of my recovery process.

When a person who has faced a crisis returns to work, people tend to think of him or her as having recovered and not still in the process of recovery. For that reason, I recommend that people do not go back on the job until they are ready to handle a full workload. The general rule that I have heard from several of my doctors is that for every day spent in the hospital, a person needs about a week of recovery time at home. Given that formula, I should have been at home recovering for 10 or 11 months. Looking back, that probably is what I needed.

I returned to work way too early, and this added to my depression. I was weak and barely out of my sickbed. I had a gaping wound in my midsection that was still healing. I was in great pain and lacked energy. I tried to step back into meetings. Several times after long stints at a conference table, I found myself on the verge of passing out. After sitting in a chair for an extended time I would feel faint, so I would lie down on the carpet. Some people thought that I wasn't engaged in the meeting. My mind wanted to interact, but my body couldn't. My spirit was willing, but my flesh was very weak.

I battled crazy hard to contribute at the same level as I had before the accident. I was trying my best to get back to my former self. I was fighting the new reality that my body had been dealt. I was trying, but I was failing miserably. And I wasn't having any fun, either.

Some people had a tough time letting go of the former Steve. They wanted the old me back. They wanted me to be Papa Bear again. I went from being the Beatles "Eight Days a Week" to not being able to do one full day of old Steve. The new Steve was walking at a slow pace and using two canes (I only needed the wheelchair for a short time). I couldn't do what I used to do. There was frustration, misunderstandings, unmet expectations and some anger. Everyone in the organization was affected.

The new reality was that I was not the same old Steve. But I was the last person to admit it. I felt lonely and abandoned. I cried every day. I listened to the Bible on CD every day. I wrote in my journal every day. Here's a typical entry:

Today I spent most of my time just holding back the tears. I feel like I am in emotional agony. I'm going forward by faith—I don't feel much of God's presence at this point. I know He loves me but I don't feel any of that right now.

My journals from that time are filled with the psalms of David. I especially honed in on David's words of hope for the future. He was often haunted by depression, and I suspect that he would have been a candidate for an antidepressant medication or two if he were alive today.

At first I resisted any medical help for my depression, but eventually I realized that I had to do something—I was quickly sinking into a black hole. I agreed to try medication and went on two prescriptions. Several years have passed since that time, and I am still on a daily regimen of medications. Some people have suggested that if I had enough faith in God, I wouldn't need any meds. "God is enough," they say. The old Steve might have said the same thing. But I have come to see that depression is not a spiritual problem; it's a physical problem. Any of us would become depressed if we lacked naturally occurring body chemicals (namely, serotonin) in our brains. We need to be smart about what we take, but we also need to be smart enough to take what we need.

Step Five: Acceptance

Once I dealt with my depression, I was ready to face my new reality. Accepting my circumstances took months and, to some degree, even years. There are aspects of my injury that have taken me a long time to figure out. For example, because part of my colon and large intestines were removed, problems related to digestion and all things colonic have come up constantly. I have daily reminders of my missing parts. It affects the way I eat meals, my energy level and the way I feel from hour to hour. I have had to learn to live with this new reality. I have had to learn to read my body and know my limits. I have also had to learn how to laugh at myself.

Like a Rolling Stone?

**WARNING: WAIT AT LEAST ONE HOUR AFTER
EATING BEFORE READING THIS NEXT STORY**

My new physical reality required a colostomy. Imagine a ziplock-type bag attached to your stomach. The bag collects whatever comes through the intestines, namely waste and gas, and can be opened at the bottom to be emptied. I couldn't predict or control this process.

During the time when I was still confined to a wheelchair, Bob Dylan came to town. He is my favorite singer of all time. I have almost all of his CDs. Janie and I needed a break, so we jumped at the chance to see this music legend. We went with our friends and fellow Dylan fans Barry and France. They graciously picked us up, took us out to dinner and got us great seats. The ushers wheeled me right up to the front—that's one benefit of being disabled!

While I was at the concert, my colostomy bag filled with gas to the point that it was about to explode. It looked like an over-inflated balloon that was attached to my stomach. Picture the guy in the movie *Alien* just before the creature popped out of his midsection. I needed to release some pressure in the colostomy bag, but I didn't want to make a scene right there in the middle of the concert.

Janie helped me during Dylan's rendition of "Like a Rolling Stone." What a wife! But when we opened the bag, whew, what a stench! People in our row couldn't figure out where the odor was coming from, but they sure knew it was pungent. Many of them were smoking marijuana, and I suspect that some thought that they had gotten some bad grass. We laid low so that no one knew I was the culprit. I wonder if Bob Dylan noticed that whole section of the audience around me was erratically doing the wave.

This was an embarrassing moment, but strange as it may sound, it was also an important one. Pardon the pun, but for me this was symbolic of really letting go of the past. It was a liberating experience, not just of the things that were building up inside of me, but also of letting go of the emotional residue that I had been hanging on to for the weeks and even months since I had gone through the injury. Letting go of the old Steve meant that I was accepting the new Steve.

On the up side, my colostomy was reversed six months later and my shortened intestines and colon were reconnected—but not before I had a little fun with it first. I had people autograph my bag (unused, of course), and found a camouflage-colored colostomy bag (the market for designer bags must be small, as that was all I could find that was creative). I can say with almost a straight face that the hard part is finding a bag to match your hat and shoes. (Okay, it's seventh-grade boy humor, but I have to laugh about my situation at least now and then.)

Letting Go

I had done a lot of living, so I had a lot of letting go to do. But it was time. For as long as I could remember, I had let other people define my self-image. When I was healthy, I thought that if people saw me as the one who was most fit, worked the longest hours and prayed for the most people, they would consider me to be the best at whatever it was I had to be best at. In many ways, I let my performance and the opinions of others define my own self-image. This didn't stop when I had my accident. I thought that if I couldn't run, jump, skip or jog, people would think I was a doofus. Simply put, I had to let go of my fear of what other people thought of me.

Our self-image needs to be determined by what God says about us, not what people say or think about us. Since my accident, I've been tempted many times to lower my self-image because of the looks that I get when I park in the handicapped spaces at the mall. People tend to cast me as a pitiable limper. I can feel their glares drilling down upon me. While I appreciate the shorter walk from the handicapped parking space, I've often thought that I would prefer walking farther than being the object of all those stares.

I've also been tempted to lower my self-image when I'm walking next to others in public spaces. When I'm traveling and

I disembark from an airplane, I often have to walk down one of those long tunnels that leads to the terminal. Because I fly so much, I often get bumped up to first class, so I am one of the first people to get off the plane. Unfortunately, I am also usually the slowest passenger, and I typically end up clogging the tunnel. It's pretty funny (or maybe sad) to see the reactions of some people. I slow them down by 30 seconds or less, but many get very antsy. Some people start to clear their throats and a few even push their way past me. I understand passengers who are in a hurry to make it to their next flight, but I seriously doubt that the few seconds they might save by flipping out is going to be of any benefit. It certainly isn't good for their blood pressure.

I had to let go of my role as the senior pastor of one of the most visible churches in America. Our church was not just the largest one in our part of Ohio, but also one of the fastest growing churches in the country. People came from far and wide to discover how we did it. Stepping down was hard because I was the lead pastor, the visionary and the go-to guy. I had to let go of the adulation that came with the job. I had to let go of the need to be looked up to by the leaders of the churches in our area. I had to let go of being respected in the community.

Transitioning out of leadership of a church that I had planted from scratch was the hardest thing I have ever done. Yet I realized that the church deserved a full-time pastor who could focus all of his energy on the work at hand. It was the right thing to do, but it hurt. It was like raising a child and having to see him or her grow away from you. It was a little like the empty-nest syndrome. What would I do next? All of the time that I spent thinking about what the church should do, where it should grow and how it should develop had to be redirected.

I had to separate my value and my worth as a person from the role that I had in the past. I had to trust that God, whose idea it was to plant the church in the first place, would have some ideas as to how it would continue to be a force in the community.

Satisfaction

Once I stepped down from visibility as the senior pastor of the church, I found great satisfaction of soul. John Wooden would call it peace of mind and peace with God. I took the time that I had and turned it to writing books. Prior to my accident I had written just two manuscripts, and those were very difficult for me to produce. After the accident, my writing came to life. For the first time I was able to sit for long periods of time and concentrate—something that is essential for writing books. I began to contact publishers with my new ideas, and they were interested. Amazon now sells 11 of my books—this will be the twelfth.

I write to motivate churches and people who want to make a difference. After my accident, I found that the key wasn't so much about being big as a church but about contentment and being the best that you can be. I quit preaching to the strong about how they could be stronger and began to speak to the weak about how they could have the courage to do what they never dreamed possible.

The things that seemed like losses in my life have turned into gains. I feel that God has redeemed what I have to offer. I am happier with my new schedule. I attend fewer meetings and use my time more wisely. I am now doing what I love and what I was designed, called and gifted to do for this season of my life.

I have found that we do not have to be hawks to soar. We know that God loves the sparrows.[2] I think that He loves the warblers, too.

Notes
1. Elisabeth Kubler-Ross, *On Death and Dying* (New York: Scribner, 1969), pp. 51-146.
2. See Matthew 10:29.

CHAPTER 7

DYING TO BE A BETTER HUSBAND

Janie and I walked along the beach and watched the Maui sun arc toward the sea. We held hands, sipped pina coladas and pondered the mystery of marriage. How was it that our relationship had endured for an amazing 25 years?

We had started our marriage with great expectations and had been through so much together. Our journey had passed through good times and not so good times. As we walked, sipped and reflected, we realized that we were not merely survivors, but that we also had synergy. We clicked—not just physically, but in all ways. Our individual gifts were more powerful in the presence of each other than they would have been had we stood alone in the world. In fact, we could not even imagine being without each other.

So why would I need to die to be a better husband? Let me count the reasons.

Janie in the Mix

Before I go any further, allow me to brag a bit about how having Janie in the mix makes things so much better.

Just today Janie and I were together helping the leadership of a church in Cincinnati—not our church, but a different one—who were rethinking their church's direction. In fact, the leadership has decided to rename and relaunch their church. I've been advising this group along the way in this process of discovery. Today, I thought to bring along Janie as an added mind. It was remarkable to see what happened between the two of us as we worked with this group of about 15 people. Janie added many helpful and practical insights. Her ideas sparked other thoughts in me, and I suggested things to the group that I wouldn't have thought to say if she hadn't been there.

That's the way it is with synergy. Two chemicals or two elements react when a third is added to the mix. In our case, I believe the third element is the presence of God.

The Bible calls King Solomon the wisest man who ever lived.[1] Solomon once said that a cord of three strands will not be quickly broken.[2] These wise words are often quoted in wedding ceremonies. I wonder if newlyweds understand what that third strand really is. They might think that it is God in general, but it's actually something much more specific than that. The third strand is always God's indwelling presence.

Far more personal than a generic God or small "g" god, we can interact with a God who is present. One way we interact with God is to wake up in the morning and ask Him for one more day of a thriving marriage. Each couple will find their own ways in which they live this out.

Some Not-So-Smart Moves

Celebrating 25 years of marriage was certainly a wonderful milestone. Janie and I had much to reflect on as we walked and sipped our pina coladas in Maui: our family, our church, our friends, our commitment to each other, the people whom we had connected with other people around the world, and much more. There had been countless good days. But life was definitely not always smooth sailing. We experienced seasons in which we lacked communication. We went through long periods during which we merely tolerated one another more than strongly loved each other.

One of the first things that God spoke to me when I was above my body in the operating room was that my marriage needed care and repair. That was no surprise to me. Janie and I had a solid marriage, but I was far from the smartest husband that God ever created. As I've already confessed, I am capable of making some incredibly dumb mistakes. Although a lot of time has come and gone since I made some of the stupidest ones, I suspect that I am still capable of making more. God help me!

Okay, I will admit to one of my not-so-smart acts. When Janie and I were newlyweds, I was annoyingly impatient. I place a high value on being punctual, especially when it comes to appointments and meetings, and I always allow enough time to get to wherever I need to go. When I did my two-year internship with the growing church in Los Angeles, our family had one car and a bicycle. (It wasn't until four years into our marriage and two children later that we added a second car.) As I mentioned, at the time we had a one-year-old girl, my daughter Rebekah.

My way to do things was to announce to Janie out of the blue that it was time to leave. I would give her all of about 10 minutes to get ready. Hey, I am a guy—who would have thought that anyone would need more time than that? I look back now and realize that I had no patience or understanding whatsoever. I can't believe how I acted. Would I ever offer to help? No! While Janie was getting Rebekah and herself ready, I would sit in the car and stare at my watch as the minutes ticked by. When it was time to be on the road, I would rev up the engine and begin to slowly drive away—as if this would speed my wife up!

Usually, Janie would somehow get into the car only a few minutes after my dumb designed departure time. Nonetheless, I would be fuming as I drove. Couldn't she understand that we needed to be on time to whatever important meeting we were headed to that day? How crazy it is that we are often at our worst when we are going to church—the place that supposedly helps us to be our best!

As thoughts of doing these things have crept back into my mind in recent years, I have gone to Janie and asked her to forgive me. As I look back, I'm amazed that our marriage endured my many unbelievable acts of stupidity. There's just no excuse for such misbehavior.

Why I Have Ears

God also nailed me regarding my ears. No, He wasn't upset about my hygiene, but He did put me on notice about my lack of using my ears to listen.

Listening is a big deal, yet it is almost a lost art. With the avalanche of media coming at us 24 hours a day, we often pay more attention to CNN, theooze.com or the cover of *People* magazine than we do to the people with whom we share our homes. Oh, we know how to talk. When it comes to human interaction, we are naturally hungry to gab away. But we mostly want to chatter about ourselves or complain about someone else.

If I was going to be effective at hearing others, I first had to learn to lay aside my own agenda. This had to start with listening to Janie. It may sound rather mindless, but the truth is that we have to empty our minds of our snappy schema if we hope to become great listeners. An agenda gets in the way of us really hearing one another. When we have a list of items that we want, that list constantly whispers in our ears while the other person is trying to share his or her heart. It gets to the point that we find it impossible to actually hear the other person's words. Our only alternative is to lay down our own agenda, or at least downsize it to a minimal list. We need to come into a conversation with the attitude of a servant.

Jesus always conducted His conversations this way. One time, He spoke with a woman at a well and asked her great questions to get to the bottom of her situation. He already intuitively knew about her situation (supernaturally), but He still asked questions and listened to her responses just the same.[3]

Great questions go hand in hand with great listening. We have to learn how to think from the other person's perspective and seek out information on what it is like to be in his or her shoes. A great question opens the door to deeper understanding. Great lawyers, philosophers and teachers communicate by asking questions. Great husbands and wives should do the same.

Sometimes, it can appear as if we are listening when we are really just formulating an answer or figuring out how to get to the next point on our agenda. Asking good questions will help us clarify what the other person is saying, but it takes effort. We need to understand the content and the emotion the person wishes to convey. Questions can lead to discovery of content, and the underlying emotion can then lead to further disclosure and understanding. I am learning that listening is less about solving problems and more about helping a person uncover what he or she actually wants to say.

We listen with our whole bodies, not just with our ears. Even though we may say that we are listening, our body language sometimes betrays us. When our arms are crossed and our eyes are looking down, it is difficult to listen well. We need to uncross our arms, make direct eye contact with the other person and relax our bodies. This will indicate that we are taking in all that he or she is saying.

Janie has always been a better listener than me. But I am improving. As I grow older, I find that I want to listen more. As I have learned to hear what Janie is saying, our marriage has grown. I have also become more effective in my work world. I believe that as we become more skilled at listening, we will be more likely to advance in our professional life. I am reminded of the proverb that says it's better to keep our mouths shut and be thought a fool than to open our mouths and erase all doubt!

I have also learned to listen by being around good listeners. My friend Dave is a professional listener. He travels around the country doing seminars on listening. I have gained much from just being Dave's friend and watching the way he interacts with his wife. But we don't need be around a professional listener to improve. There are good listeners all around. We each should make it a point to spend time with people who are skilled in this area and ask them questions about how they learned to listen. Some people are naturals, but most aren't. I ask good listeners what motivates them. Their enthusiasm always rubs off.

An excellent book on listening is *Quick to Listen Leaders*, written by Dave Ping and Anne Clippard, two great listeners and trainers. In this book, the authors explore thoughtful and engaging ways to communicate warmth, empathy and respect. No matter what stage of life or employment we are in, we all can benefit from some concerted effort to grow as listeners.

Why I Say Thanks

Whew! Enough of my not-so-hot stuff, already! Since my accident, I have become a more grateful person, and I can honestly say that I have not grown tired of saying thanks. When I was barreling through life and could do much for myself, I didn't notice when others did things for me. I did not say thank you often enough. I thought that just saying thanks every now and then was enough to cover all the bases. But truthfully, I needed to cultivate an attitude of thankfulness.

I am thankful that Janie stood by me throughout this whole ordeal. She spent every day and most nights with me in the hospital. She was my arms and legs when I couldn't get around very easily. She emptied the colostomy bag made famous at the Dylan concert and occasionally had to change the sheets in the middle of the night when it blew up without warning. For a while, she was my connection to the outside world. She had to keep a lot of plates spinning at the same time.

I am thankful for all of our friends who helped Janie with the kids and the house. They brought meals over, made Christmas happen while I was away and supported us in so many other ways. I am thankful for the prayers that were prayed (and continue to be prayed) for God's purposes to be fulfilled in me and through my family.

A thankful heart lifts our own life and the lives of those around us. A thankful heart puts us in a positive frame of mind—we automatically look on the bright side of things and don't have to work so hard at being positive. A good attitude comes more easily when we walk in thankfulness.

People who are continually thankful are a joy to be around. "Thank therapy" is the way to go. I now say thanks to people for just about anything they offer to do for me. When I go to a restaurant, I go out of my way to make sure that I thank the server (after all, it's a pretty thankless job to do). When I sign my credit card receipt, I always write an encouraging note to him or her, such as, "Thanks for the fantastic service!" Then I leave a generous tip— usually about 30 percent. Wherever I speak, I always attempt to mention that part of living generously is tipping well. It is one sign of a thankful heart. Thankfulness is the way that I want to live my life. It's contagious and life-giving.

Having an attitude of thankfulness changes the way in which we relate to others. We treat others differently and behave in a more cheerful way around them. I have found that when I thank God on a daily basis for Janie, my gratefulness grows and I am more positive toward her.

Of course, I still have to work on my attitude at times. I am a somewhat cynical person by nature, but my attitude improves more quickly when I have a thankful heart. The main thing for me is to watch my heart. If my heart is clean, I do life with excellence!

More Turtle Stuff

These days, I move slower emotionally and walk slower physically. My metronome is set at a different pace than before. Since my accident, I can't help but stop to smell the roses.

My legs are long for my height. When I was in high school, my jeans were size 30-inch waist and 36-inch length. Those are some long legs, even for a guy who is 6 feet 2 inches tall. I usually had to special order my pants.

I've always had a long, fast gait. For the first few years of our marriage, Janie could barely keep up with me when we would go for a walk. With my lack of sensitivity, I never thought of slowing down a bit in order to let her catch up. I just charged full steam ahead! There was no time for holding hands. Sometimes we resembled a family from India, with the husband walking 15 paces ahead of his wife and kids. But in our case, the pace wasn't for the sake of honor. It was just another mark of my impatience. Now the tables have turned. Janie walks faster than I do. I limp along at a slow pace and ask her to slow down so that I can catch up.

A few years ago, I was invited to speak at a Billy Graham training event in Amsterdam. One day, Janie, my mother and I were walking around the city to see the sights. It was late afternoon, and Janie and my mom got to talking and wandered quite a bit ahead of me. As I limped along with my cane on the cobblestone streets of the old city, I soon realized that my wife and my mother were almost out of shouting distance.

We didn't realize it at the time, but we had accidentally wandered into Amsterdam's red light district. Prostitution is legal in Amsterdam, and the girls are displayed in windows with literal red lights shining down on them. They are like wares for sale at Bloomingdale's. Unintentionally, I looked the part of a customer: I was a middle-aged American man strolling in front of the windows, seemingly alone. When I realized how bad this looked, I called out, "Hey, wait for me!" to Janie and my mom.

Wow, how things have flip-flopped completely. But Janie is much kinder than I ever was. She is only too happy to walk at my pace. More important, our emotional pace is now in sync. We are now equally matched. The hope of our lives is that we have the same general goals. We negotiate on the big deals and give freedom to one another on the little ones. And, thus, we move along in the same direction and to the same cadence.

A Perfect Match

I don't hold to the idea that there is just one person out there for each of us and that it should be our quest to find that perfect match. Rather, I think that there could be quite a few prospective mates who could be a good a fit for us.

In preparation for marriage, our job is to explore life widely and to get to know many members of the opposite gender. Of course, we naturally will want to show our best side, not only when it comes to attracting a mate, but also in any social situation. But we will also need to humble ourselves. If we are not real, we will ultimately be frustrated, falling in love with one person during courtship only to discover a totally different person during the first year of marriage. I have worked with singles and newlyweds for decades and have found this to be a common pattern.

A groom should consider his bride the love of his life and the best thing that ever happened to him. He should be her soul mate and treat her as his true love no matter what emotions come and go. A bride should view her husband-to-be in the same way.

Relationships are never stagnant. Like it or not, they have atmosphere. They are always headed in one direction or another. As much as we would like to think of a marriage as something that can run on its own steam, in reality we need to put forth an effort each day. The grass is not greener on the other side of the fence—or on the other side of whatever emotional pitfall we allow to drag us down. The grass is greener where we water it.

Obviously, I am only offering up a few points that Janie and I have learned. Every single person and every couple needs to know as much as possible about what makes good relationships. Many insightful books have been written about courtship and marriage—read them! I wish I had. (Perhaps I will write one just on relationships one day!)

Two Couples

Janie and I enjoy watching people. A while back we were out to dinner and noticed two couples. One had apparently been married for a long, unhappy time. The other couple was newly wed.

The husband and wife in the long-term marriage were obviously not enjoying each other's company that night, and we suspected that they had not had any nights out for a long time. They sat through their entire meal without saying a single word to one another—seriously, not even to ask, "How's the steak?"

The two made no eye contact with each other that we could detect. They might as well have just blended up their meal and drank it for all the joy that they were getting out of the experience. It was almost painful to watch them.

Janie and I guessed that long ago this husband and wife had established some marital rules, but that they had then proceeded to break those rules so many times that all they had left between them was disappointment. They probably should have divorced a long time ago, but neither of them went to the trouble of going to a lawyer to put an official end to their years of misery. Perhaps they were sticking it out for the sake of their children. From all the signals they put out, it was apparent that they didn't have a marriage—they had a standoff.

The man and woman in the other couple were no doubt in their first year of marriage. Their rings were bright and shiny. They talked nonstop and their laughing and leg-slapping even interrupted Janie and I as we tried to talk. It seemed to the husband that everything his bride said was hilarious. He said in a loud voice, "You really ought to go into stand-up comedy!" He was so happy that he was almost crying.

To the woman, it seemed that everything her groom said was incredibly wise. She was actually taking notes on her napkin! She kept saying, "I've never thought of it that way." They maintained strong eye contact—when the waiter brought their food, they didn't even look at him. They just said thanks and kept gabbing on.

These two couples are living proof of the fact that relationships are always headed in one direction or another. Couples, whether they are dating or married, are either going toward a place of healing or are fragmenting apart. They are never marching in place.

Jesus said that we are either for Him or against Him—there is no middle ground.[4] In the same way, our actions will either help or hurt our marriage. There is no *Oh, that didn't matter.*

Soul Mates and Dates

I look forward to going out on dates with Janie—more so now than before we were married. Why? Because I know her better and realize the treasure that I have. Simply put, I enjoy spending time with Janie more now than I did then.

We don't just go some place romantic, hold hands and stare at one another. No, we do a variety of things. Both of us are movie buffs, so we often take in a flick. We take turns picking which movie we will see. She likes romantic comedies, while I like action thrillers. However, it doesn't really matter what we see. I just get a kick out of being with Janie for a couple of hours in the dark!

After the movie, we usually go out to dinner, have ice cream or get a cup of coffee. We talk about the movie. We judge its high points and low points. We compare the actors' performances to their roles in previous films. We rate the movie from one to five stars. Move over Ebert and Roeper—here comes Steve and Janie!

God does exist! How else could you explain two humans being so supremely happy and alive to the fullest in one another's company—and for more than 25 years! When we celebrated our anniversary this year, we didn't go whole hog and travel to Hawaii. We kept it pretty low key. In fact, one of us wasn't feeling well on our actual anniversary evening, so we delayed our celebration for a few days. We simply went out to eat and spent several hours reflecting on the highlights of our years together. We laughed a lot and even cried a little.

I think that's the goal of marriage—to be able to be best friends. The reward of marriage is just to be with the other person. It's beyond the joy of sex, though that is part of the equation. It's not winning discussions or arguments. Those of us who have traveled beyond the surface into the mystery of marriage know that it is all about coming to the place of peace with ourselves and the one who is so close to us that we can call him or her our soul mate.

I have discovered much, but now more than ever I am dying to be an even better soul mate to Janie. I look forward to taking another walk with her, watching another Maui sunset, and reflecting back on 50 years of marriage.

Notes
1. See 1 Kings 3:12.
2. See Ecclesiastes 4:23.
3. See John 4:7-30.
4. See Luke 11:23.

DYING TO BE A BETTER FATHER

Daydream with me for a moment. I walk into the local Barnes and Noble (or maybe it is Borders or Books-A-Million). Moving past the bestsellers and new arrivals, I head toward the magazine racks. I am looking for the latest motorcycle monthly, but the cover of *Modern Bride* catches my eye. As every father does, I have anticipated the day when I will walk my daughters down the aisle.

I can picture myself in a tuxedo and Rebekah (and later, Laura) in a spectacular white and ivory gown with a snowflake rhinestone headpiece and veil. As we saunter in from the back of the chapel, we see the crowd of family and friends that has gathered. Everyone is so happy. Waiting up front, of course, is my future son-in-law. In my daydream, I do not recognize him, but I have been praying for him for years. Even before our daughters were born, Janie and I would ask God to bring along the right man at the right time for each daughter. So far, everything is perfect.

My gaze moves from the groom to the bridal party. These are Rebekah's (and later, Laura's) best friends. I start to smile, but then I realize that something is amiss. I recognize a few of the bridesmaids, but the others do not look familiar. What's worse, I don't know *any* of their names! In fact, I don't know the names of any of my daughter's friends who have come to celebrate her wedding day! Ouch.

Thankfully, this is only a daydream—if it had occurred at night, it would have a more ominous name. And thankfully, when I do walk my daughters down the aisle, this scenario will not happen. But it could have.

Know Thy Children's Friends

God got me good. I was hovering over the operating table as close to the ceiling as I could get without actually leaving the room. The doctors were in emergency mode and God was calmly quizzing me. "Do you know the names of your children's friends?" He asked. This was not a daydream. God wanted to know the answer, but I couldn't list a single one! I was caught dead to rights.

The realization struck me like a bolt of lightning. I hadn't taken the time to get to know my children's best friends and long-term buddies, yet alone the new classmate Laura had brought over a few weeks earlier. My oversight was embarrassing and inexcusable. These friends often visited our house. They were always welcome, but I was anything but hospitable. When they came, I was usually fixated on one project or another. Many times, I just wasn't there. My job was important, after all.

While working hard is good, being totally immersed in work to the point of excluding family members is a fatal error. I found out the hard way. In my case, this error was not terminal, but it was a close call.

Since that day in the operating room, I have gone to my children—all three of them—and asked each one to forgive me. I've told them that I was not an example of a good father, much less a good pastor.

The Pretty Good Father

Since my accident, I have often mulled over ideas on what it would take to be a great father—or at least a pretty good one. Hopefully, what I have learned will help all fathers, especially those who have found themselves on the merry-go-round of working too much and not paying enough attention to their children.

If children have an incorrect or cracked view of their father, they will ultimately have an incorrect or cracked view of God. Perhaps this explains a lot about the world in which we live.

Pretend for a moment that today is the last day of your life. You are dying of cancer and will kick the bucket at midnight. How will you approach your children during this day? I suspect that you will carefully measure each step, if not each word. You will want to be remembered in a certain way. Of course, living this way before you die is like faking love before you get married.

Anyone can put on a show for a certain length of time, but if given more time, everyone goes back to old habits. Unfortunately, this can happen in a parent-child relationship. Once a father has captured the affections of his offspring, he tends to let himself go until something traumatic happens. Only when the child overdoses on crack or the father faces losing his job do the alarms start to sound.

Unfortunately, it took a near-fatal experience to get my attention. That's tragic. I blew it. Don't be as blind as I was. Make a determined effort to be a better father.

You may ask (as I did), *Why can't we just read about someone else's mismanagement of life and then let that be a lesson to us?* Why can't we just read this book and then never make another mistake? (I write this with a knowing nod.) A few of us may be able to read and avoid these pitfalls, but most will be like me and have to live and learn.

Pipes Not Pans

At this point, I want to offer just a few things that I have learned about being a pretty good father, beginning with generosity.

Before my accident, I wasn't necessarily a miser. I gave good Christmas presents to my kids. I gave decent birthday gifts, too. But I wasn't generous. There is a difference between merely giving a present and living a life of generosity.

Being generous does not mean that we must be rich. Many people with moderate means are openhanded. Generous people are creative and energetic. They know that generosity is not as much a matter of how much is in their wallets as it is of how big their hearts are. A charitable heart will shine over and over again, and our children will notice.

We can ask ourselves, *Do we want to be remembered as a generous person?* If so, we need to hold on to our goods and money loosely, no matter how much we have or do not have. We need to let things flow through our life to avoid becoming containers or collectors. One practice that I have taken up since my injury is giving great amounts of money to my children on their birthdays. I multiply my age times their age and give them that multiple. As I age and they grow older, the pot grows. My son, Jack, who is still a teenager under 18, gets a sizeable sum each July. (By the way, I stop the practice when the child reaches 18.)

This formula may not be possible for some people. That is fine. Perhaps some people will divide their age by one-half and then give their children that multiple. Others may simply increase the cost of a gift by a few dollars each year. Remember, it is not the amount that matters but the attitude in which it is given.

Some people might think that I'm a little extravagant, but I don't think so. I believe that my children will never forget my attempts to bless them. Not surprisingly, they often buy gifts for others with part of the money that they receive. They allow the money to flow through them, which makes me smile.

I like to picture my life as being that of a pipe, not of a pan. A pipe is a channel through which things can pass to give life-giving nourishment to others. A pan, on the other hand, is a receptacle that only collects things. It represents a one-way flow. Stuff comes into a pan, but it never goes out.

Money and possessions are not the only gifts that we can give to our children. We can also give them our love, and we can do so in different ways. Some people find that words are the best means for expressing the language of love. Others prefer using touch as the means for sending a message that says "I love you." No matter how we say it, we need to lavish love upon our children from the moment they are born until the day we breathe our last breath.

Perhaps many of us feel that we have blown it with our kids—that we have not done such a bang-up job in showing love or in being generous with them. In fact, many people whom I have talked to over the years feel that they have done irreparable damage to their parent-child relationship. They have reached the point of despair. This feeling comes to a head as their children finish high school and begin to move out on their own. Many parents throw up their hands in the air and say, "What's the use—I've done so much wrong, why even try to make any changes."

As an imperfect parent who has made my fair share of mistakes, I can attest to the fact that it's *never* too late to start again. It may take some humility on our part, but we can always go back to our children. Our offspring may be resistant at first, but we must press forward. Children are fairly resilient. They can bounce back from years of poor modeling once a parent asks for forgiveness and then begins to change his or her own behavior.

Our Miracle Hamster

My daughter Laura wanted a hamster. I was happy just watching the squirrels in our backyard, but she was persistent. I warned Laura that a hamster would have baby hamsters (a million of them), escape from its cage, scamper around in the attic, and bite her fingers! The truth was that I just didn't want a rodent in the house—not even a cute caged one.

This happened long before my accident, but I tell the story here because it is a perfect example of how I needed to learn how to actually listen to my children instead of simply placating them. Laura pleaded, prodded and pouted. She wanted that hamster! Finally, I gave in—not because I wanted her to be happy, but because she had worn me out. Wrong reason, I know, but it happens. Ask any parent.

Laura was beaming when we brought the hamster home. I rolled my eyes, but I held my tongue. On day two in the Sjogren zoo, we discovered that the hamster was pregnant! Before I could say "I told you so," we had eight little ones. Thankfully, we were able to find eight suckers—uh . . . I mean nice families—who were willing to take in the little baby hamsters to bite the fingers of their children. (I told you that my attitude wasn't so hot on this one.)

Now for the great escape. Yes, the hamster got out of its cage. No, it didn't head for the attic; it went straight for the closet, gnawing its way through several inches of brand new carpet!

Laura's cute little $4 pet cost us $100 in repairs.

That was the second strike, but the hamster eventually won our sympathy. One day, we noticed a growth on the hamster's body. It was cancerous, but we didn't have the heart to commit hamster euthanasia. Remarkably, the little hamster survived for many years. We called her our miracle pet. (By the way, she never bit Laura's finger or did any of the other things that I had predicted.)

As parents, we need to listen to our children and actually consider what they are saying to us. We need to hear them out instead of just giving in to them because we don't want to deal with the situation. When I bought the hamster for Laura, I did so because I allowed myself to be worn down by her pestering me. This doesn't mean that I wouldn't eventually have gotten the hamster anyway, but just that I should have taken the time to really listen to my daughter and make a wise and informed decision. In fact, if you get me on a good day, I will admit that even I had a little affection for the rodent. But after that, we stuck to dogs as pets.

Flexible Fatherhood

I have learned to be flexible with my children, even though that is not my first reaction when challenges come my way.

Jesus once spoke a series of beatitudes in a sermon. These beatitudes all start out with the word "blessed." You've probably heard the famous verse, "Blessed are the meek, for they shall inherit the earth."[1] I have invented another beatitude. It's not in the Bible, but it sure is true to life: "Blessed are the flexible, for they shall bend and not be broken." If you are a parent, you know the truth of that one!

I have a tendency to tense up when I see an infraction occurring in my children's lives. This is especially true in the life of my first-born child, Rebekah. She tends to get the stiffest treatment. As with most families, we place high expectations upon the performance of our firstborn.

I remember when my daughter as a teenager wore a bikini to the beach for the first time. I flipped out. I was superprotective. "That's too revealing," I said. "Get covered up. That's ridiculous. Get a one-piece bathing suit. I'll pick it out for you, in fact." I had something in mind from the mid-1950s.

My daughter was wearing a suit that looked like the ones that all of the others girls on the beach were wearing—it wasn't out of line. It wasn't *that* revealing, actually. I just hadn't crossed that bridge with her, and I overreacted. A large part of the problem was that I hadn't taken the time to sit down to listen to my daughter and then negotiate with her about the bikini. I hadn't spoken to her about the whole topic of modesty versus being cool. If I had, I would have heard her side and been more understanding.

It's interesting how Janie and I have different levels of flexibility. By nature, Janie is much more emotionally limber. She is from Southern California, where most people are laid back. She was raised near the surf. Picture the Beach Boys doing their most vibrant rendition of "Ba-Ba-Ba-Ba-Ba-Barbara Ann"—that's my wife!

It was good that Janie was flexible in the early years of our parenting, because she brought balance into our teamwork as a duo over our children. Without her, I would have caused the kids to go into counseling at an early age!

Respect from Elders

I have also learned to be more respectful of my children. As parents, we are more used to the idea of reminding our children to respect us rather than us respecting them, but I think that it works both ways. Almost anyone can be a parent of a child, but it takes a strong individual to respect that child throughout his or her life.

This is yet another area in which I failed to shine as a parent. I didn't lack respect for my children, but I was so busy with work that I failed to communicate to them through my life that I had a high degree of respect for their lives.

For example, I have not thought that all of my daughters' choices of boyfriends have exactly been terrific. Every father feels strongly about protecting his daughters from low-life guys, and this is especially true when boys first start to show up on the scene. None of them are good enough. They are all lowlifes!

I made intimidating the boys who came to our house a fine art. I would have them shaking in their boots when I got through with them. My daughters later told me that their dates were no fun after I got through grilling them. My daughters would probably say that I skewered their dates. I could always find a fault.

After my accident, I realized that I was doing my daughters a disservice. I could no longer justify my intrusion into their dating lives. I am still watchful and very willing to share my opinions, but their boyfriends no longer have to fill out a 20-page questionnaire, pass a lie detector test and have their hair examined for head lice. Now I am more respectful. I greet Rebekah's and Laura's dates with open arms and engage them in friendly conversation. I even learn their names! I realize that these young men aren't out to harm my daughters. I believe that they have my daughters' best interest in mind. Most important, I now trust my daughters' ability to judge men.

One day, I will walk Rebekah and Laura down the aisle. I will wear a tuxedo and they will wear lovely white dresses. We will be beaming as we saunter toward the front of the chapel. Family and friends will all be gathered. That will be a day of both sadness and rejoicing for me—sadness in that my daughters are going off on their own, but rejoicing in that we have gained a son-in-law and extended our family. The prayers that we prayed for our daughters before they were born will have been answered. And I will know my new sons-in-law's names!

Note
1. See Matthew 5:5.

Chapter 9

DYING TO BE A BETTER FRIEND

Osborne and I have been best friends for 20 years. We were at Starbucks the other day, drinking coffee and laughing. It's scary to think how many gallons of coffee we have consumed while talking about everything from our families to our work to our dreams. Osborne was there for me when I had problems with some of my staff. He was there when we bought the miracle hamster for Laura. And he was there when I was in the hospital. Osborne has stood by me on both my good days and my bad days. I could not ask for a better friend. Yet I found that I could have been a better friend to him and to others. Like most things in my life, I learned the hard way.

A Generous Friendship

One definition of a friend is someone who is an acquaintance. Before my accident, I was always around people and had lots of acquaintances. If you had asked me, I would have told you that I also had many rock-solid and deep friendships—and even a few lifelong ones. To a point that was true, but it took my face-to-face encounter with God in the operating room to convince me that when it came to friendship, I had only just scratched the surface.

I previously wrote about the lineup of people who came to visit me at the hospital. As I mentioned, most of these people were friendly, but some lugged their unresolved issues with me into the room. And there were certainly boatloads of people who did not come to my bedside that also clung to residue of unresolved conflicts with me.

I knew about some of the problems but didn't think too much about any of them. *Offenses, mistakes, misunderstandings—they happen,* I reasoned. *Every leader has "those types of people" floating around in their life. Time was better spent building new friendships instead of trying to salvage old broken-down ones.* On one occasion before my accident another pastor called me on this attitude, but I was stubborn in my ways and didn't change.

In hindsight, I realize that my perspective was skewed. I've now done an about-face and think that it is best to walk clean before man and God at all times. In other words, if I offend someone or if someone blasts me, I make every effort to mend the gaffe—preferably before the sun goes down. When it comes to putting forth the effort to make friendships right, I think that we can afford to be generous with our time.

A New Kind of Friend

In using the phrase "a new kind of," I realize that I am spinning off from the title of a popular book by Brian McLaren.[1] But I consider Brian to be a friend—and besides, it works! As a new kind of friend, I found that I needed to adjust my behavior as well as my attitude. So in this chapter, in my ADD style, I am going to cover an array of concepts and practices about friendships. Believe it or not, some of these came as revelations to me. I have found that they all work.

So, what is a friend? Well, the Sjogren dictionary defines a friend as a person who keeps a short list of wrongs, tells you immediately about grievances and then lets them go. He or she stands by you through thick and thin but confronts you when something you've said or done isn't right. A friend allows you to vent on your bad days, act silly on your good days, or even be silent on days that you have nothing to say. A friend encourages you to pursue your dreams and then celebrates your victories when you achieve those dreams. He or she picks up the tab at Starbucks (at least every other time), finds the time to call or e-mail you when there is no time, and checks in on you regularly. A friend assumes the best in you and doesn't believe everything that he or she hears about you from others.

My friend Osborne is an African-American pastor who was born in Ghana. He fits this definition perfectly. We get together at least once a month for a few hours, usually to have lunch and talk from the heart. We exchange thoughts about our fears, our hopes and our aspirations. If I have been to some place interesting, I fill him in. If his family has done something wild or profound, he lets me know. If I have pondered something perplexing in my journal, I discuss this with him. Osborne and I pray together and then report back to each other on how God has answered those prayers.

Osborne was a faithful friend throughout my health crisis. I cannot count the times and the ways that he encouraged me. His mother lifted me up during this time as well. At first glance, Osborne's mother is not someone with whom you would think I would naturally connect. Thankfully, first glances do not always tell the whole story.

Not long after she heard about my accident, this elderly woman from Ghana prophesied that I would survive if I made it through the first night in the ICU. When I was still around the next morning, Osborne was absolutely jubilant. Although I remained in critical condition, Osborne was absolutely beaming. I looked as good as dead, but he was ecstatic and announced to everyone that I was going to make it.

Osborne's declaration about my future was similar to the antithesis of the news of Mark Twain's demise. Folklore has it that while Mark Twain was still very much alive, a newspaper ran his obituary. When Twain heard about the report, he retorted that "news of my death has been greatly exaggerated," or something along those lines. In my case, my obituary was ready to run, but Osborne was telling everyone that God was not reading it. It was a hard message to swallow given the mesh of tubes strung into my body like lights hung haphazardly on a Christmas tree, but Osborne was insistent.

Beyond the Earthly Plane

One of my first memories upon waking up from my induced coma was that of Osborne standing by my bed. In his Ghanese accent (it sounds a bit like French), he almost shouted: "Great news! Big things lie ahead for you. I can hardly wait to take you to the mall. I am going to buy you a pair of Cole Hahn shoes." For some reason, Osborne had it in his head that he was supposed to buy me a new pair of shoes to celebrate my recovery. I, however, felt as if a Mack truck had just hit me. Every bit of my body was in pain. Even my toes hurt.

> *It is not events that disturb the minds of men, but the view they take of them.*
>
> —Epictetus

I love books that throw in apropos quotes at unexpected moments. I cite Epictetus here because his words remind me of Osborne's actions during that time. Osborne did not look at the physical mess strewn before him in that suburban ICU ward. Instead, he looked with the eyes of faith, hope and expectation. Osborne was stoked as he viewed what was beyond the earthly plane.

Over the next few months, as I was transferred to two other hospitals and then sent home to recover, Osborne came by every day. He even visited me when I didn't want him to be there. He was by my side when I went through a period in which I wanted to give up—a time I call my "crying phase." I asked him to stay away, but he ignored my request. I tried to chase him off, but he was stubborn and came back day after day.

It is easy to be a friend when things are going good, but not many people will stand by us when the flow of life is going against us. This is particularly true when death is nearby. We've all had friends who abandon us when we are down. These types of people are really just acquaintances, not friends. Osborne is the antithesis. He is the kind of friend we all want and hope for.

In the movie *Forrest Gump*, there is a scene in which Forrest is fighting in the Vietnam War and rescues some soldiers from his platoon during an attack. His leader, Lieutenant Dan, has his legs blown off and is dying in the jungle. But Forrest risks his life and runs back to where Lieutenant Dan has fallen. He carries Lieutenant Dan out of harm's way just moments before napalm falls onto the jungle where they had been fighting. Lieutenant Dan is furious with Forrest for saving him and even asks to be taken back to the jungle so that he can die on the battlefield.

During my crisis, I was like Lieutenant Dan and Osborne was like Forrest Gump. I wanted to be left behind to die, at least emotionally, and I argued with my rescuer. I treated Osborne like dirt and told him to leave me alone. I sometimes even turned my head toward the corner of the room. But Osborne just smiled and kept encouraging me.

Osborne not only encouraged me with his words but also practiced a wonderful form of listening. He allowed me to talk, even when all I had to say was nonsense. He was a selective listener, patiently waiting for me to finish with my baloney so that we could get to the real matters on my heart. Having someone who wanted to help me resurrect my best intentions was a healing kind of listening.

Osborne prayed for me and with me. One of the strongest ways to express loving concern for another person is to pray for him or her. Regardless of whether we understand prayer or have a strong belief in it, everyone around us will grow powerfully when we pray. In the 30 years that I have spent in offering prayer to people, no one has ever turned me down. There's something in the human heart that cries out for prayer and getting in touch with God.

The Risk of Vulnerability

Friendship can save a person or a community, but there are risks. To be a rock-solid friend, it takes being vulnerable and being real. On our good days, we will all look good—but then there are those bad days. A friend will help us get over the speed bumps and will look past the dumb things that we might do or say. Let me explain.

Have you ever had a friend work against you? I have. On one occasion, I thought that I was telling a particular person something in complete confidence. Actually, I was venting. The words that I said to the person were emotional and reactionary, but I thought that they would be quickly forgotten—in one ear and out the other. After all, I had dismissed similar off-the-wall things that the other person had said to me in the past. I figured that everybody deserves to have a bad day now and then. It seemed unfair to hold people to something that they might have said during one of these bad days in their lives.

In my case, I discovered that years after my venting, what I thought was confidential had been carefully logged and remembered *word for word*. Although I didn't realize it at the time, I had been giving a deposition. When I was at my most vulnerable point—after my accident—my words would come back to bite me. They were used as weapons against me to make me look foolish and even hypocritical. And all of this came from someone whom I had considered to be a good friend! Was I ever wrong.

After being burned, it took me a while to get back to the place of being able to trust people and open up to them in more than casual sharing. I finally came to realize that it would be tragic to allow an incident or two such as this to put me in a place in which I could no longer open up my soul to another friend. We are all designed to dialogue with others. That's what community is all about. If we can't trust others, something starts to die within us and we become unable to connect with them.

I understand how this all works because I've done something similar. On rare occasions, Janie or I will bring up old issues that have long since passed under the bridge and use those issues against each other. I have fallen into the trap of turning confidential information against a person, but I know that it isn't right or best.

I've discovered that sometimes when people come across as super nice, they are actually keeping a record of rights and wrongs. When people seem too good to be true, they usually are.

Oh, the comfort, the inexpressible comfort of feeling safe with a person; having neither to weigh thoughts nor measure words, but to pour them all out, just as they are, chaff and grain together, knowing that a faithful hand will take and sift them, keep what is worth keeping, and then, with a breath of kindness, blow the rest away.

—George Eliot

If we don't want to damage our relationships, we need to learn how to hold on to our friendships but let go of our grievances.

It's a tricky thing to deal with past hurts. On the one hand, the old adage "live and learn" is absolutely true. When someone hurts us, we are wiser for it and don't want to again fall into the original trap that led to the hurt. For example, if a person betrays a confidence, you would be wise to not confide in him or her at such a deep level again because that person has demonstrated that he or she is incapable of handling interpersonal matters. However, if a prolonged period of time passes and you believe that the person has acquired new interpersonal skills, you may feel that it is again safe to share something deep with him or her once again. Step out onto the ice and take the risk. Relationships are based on risks.

Lessons on Forgiveness

Becoming a better friend means becoming a better forgiver. Although I'm struggling right along with every person reading this and am not an expert on the topic, I have picked up a few tips on forgiveness over the years. The topic of forgiveness is so dynamic that I'm constantly learning new lessons on how to walk it out in my day-to-day life.

The rule of reprimand is that you have only thirty seconds to share your feelings. And when it's over, it's over.

—Ken Blanchard

When we forgive, we give up the right to again bring up the past grievance in conversation. This is not the same as forgive and forget—it's impossible to forget a hurtful experience that we've gone through because our memories are indelibly marked by hurtful episodes in our pasts. We can forgive a person in an absolutely healthy way and still have vivid memories of that hurt.

In many ways, it's actually a good thing to remember the hurtful things that have happened to us. We can learn from the past and hopefully not repeat our mistakes as we go forward into our improved futures. We can chalk up negative experiences to our youth, inexperience, poor communication skills, unexpressed expectations and other causes of hurtful experiences that damage our emotions.

However, if we just dwell on the hurt, we haven't truly forgiven the other person. The act of forgiveness means being generous to others in order to allow our emotions to heal. It means that even though they don't deserve it, we are going to give our forgiveness to them—we take the "for" and then add the "give."

We must forgive so that all of the negative emotion connected to the hurt doesn't fester inside of us. I know all about things festering inside. I once went to Poland to speak at a conference and contracted a stomach infection that lasted for more than four months—that's a lot of festering! I had a low-grade fever and lacked energy. My symptoms are a good analogy for what happens when we fail to forgive. We become drained and sick with a full body fever. It affects our very soul. We don't sleep properly and are constantly upset in the pit of our emotions until resolution comes about.

So how do we actually begin the process of forgiving others for the hurt that they have caused us in the past? First, go *quickly* to the person to make things right. Don't wait for the person who has wronged you to bring up the subject. If you wait, the conflict may well never be resolved. Second, seek forgiveness for your *own* sake, not for the *other person's* sake. In a way, forgiveness is a supremely selfish act!

My mom struggled for years with forgiveness following the breakup of her marriage to my stepdad. All of the symptoms brought about by the lack of forgiveness plagued her for a long time. Then one day she experienced a breakthrough—she realized that she was tired of living beneath her potential. My mom decided to deal with her issues of forgiveness. Since that time, she has been at peace with herself and her life.

Joyous Messes

We all have issues with forgiveness. What are yours? Are you willing to deal honestly with your matters of the heart? How about beginning today?

If you go by your feelings, you will be a roller coaster of emotions—forgiving now and then not forgiving the next time an emotionally charged event enters your life. You have to develop the habit of forgiveness. You have to make a commitment to live a lifestyle of forgiveness. It's something you have to decide to walk in each day.

To paraphrase the Bible, we should "count it all joy when we have lots of trials and people to forgive," because that means we have lots of relationships.[2] God has put a lot of people around us who love us. Yes, it's going to be a bit messy (count on it!), but that's better than the alternative—not having anyone to call our friend and living out our days in a sterile and lifeless environment. I'll take messy over empty any time.

Notes

1. See Brian McLaren, *A New Kind of Christian: A Tale of Two Friends on a Spiritual Journey* (Hoboken, NJ: Jossey-Bass, 2001).
2. See James 1:2.

CHAPTER 10

DYING TO BE EVEN KINDER

When Janie and I arrived at the Vineyard Community Church in Cincinnati, the church tried various traditional methods of doing outreach in the community. After two years, we were averaging around 30 people at our Sunday services. It was at this point that we decided to try something a bit more radical—something I termed "servant outreach."

The concept immediately took off and our church began to grow. Soon, pastors from various churches in the area began visiting to see what we were doing so that they could implement it in their churches. When they asked me the secret to servant outreach, I was only too glad to share it with them. "Let's go to the restaurant across town," I would say.

Thinking that we were going to the restaurant to talk, the pastors were quite surprised when, after entering the restaurant, I proceeded to the restroom with cleaning supplies in hand. For the next half hour or so, my guest and I would scrub each of the toilets by hand. That was servant outreach. Sometimes we would hand out bottles of water on hot days, shovel snow on cold days, paint houses, put quarters in the washing machines at the laundromat or wash people's cars. Serving the community became contagious. I even wrote a book about it titled *Conspiracy of Kindness*.

Now, after all that I have been through with my accident, people ask me if I still believe in the power of kindness to change the world. Unequivocally, I always state that I do. In fact, I believe in the power of kindness even more strongly now than I ever did before.

Scattering the Seeds

One of the big differences in me since my accident is that I now have a looser grip on things than before. I love to give things away. Before the accident, I was afraid that if I gave too much away, things would get out of control. I thought that I would end up not knowing when to stop giving and that I would go bankrupt. Now I realize that giving is supposed to be out of our control—on a regular basis! And so far, I haven't gone bankrupt.

One of my driving passions is to help people know God, and I believe that they will be more open to wanting to know God when they are shown kindness. I also don't believe that just one act of kindness will do it. In the parable of the sower, Jesus spoke of the farmer who went out and threw seeds all over the place. He threw seeds on rocky ground, shallow ground, thorny ground and on ground with good soil. The different types of soil in Jesus' parable represented the different stages of readiness in people to receive God's love. But the farmer didn't judge which portion of the ground was worthy to receive the seed. He just generously and lavishly spread it everywhere.

In the natural, I am not necessarily a kind person. But I live my life with an eye to continually finding ways to extend kindness. It's the kindness of God, not the kindness of Steve. For example, sometimes I go through the drive-thru at Taco Bell and ask the guy at the window how much the person's tab is behind me (it's usually less than $4—isn't Taco Bell great!). I pay the bill and give the guy in the window a simple card that reads "This is to show you God's love in a practical way, with no strings attached!" The phone number of our church is printed on the back of the card so that the person can call if he or she wants to follow up on that act of kindness. Then I simply drive away. I don't wait for a thank-you or to see the look of surprise on the face of the person (though that would be fun!).

I do this almost every time I'm at a Taco Bell, Wendy's, Arby's, McDonald's or any other fast-food restaurant. If there is a drive-thru window, I'm on it. I even do it at Starbucks. "What kind of drink are you ordering this morning?" I will ask the person in line behind me. He or she often looks a little surprised.

"Why are you asking?"

"Oh, I'm just in a generous mood this morning," I say, "and I'd like to buy your drink."

"That's all right, I'll buy my own . . ." The person always—and I mean *always*—responds this way.

"No really, let me do it," I reply. "It will do my heart good to give something away today. Please let me buy your drink for you." The person usually relents at this point. But I'm not quite finished yet.

"I believe it's much better to give away than to receive," I then say. This often elicits a strange look.

"What kind of a person are you anyway?!"

"I just love to give things away. I've received a lot in life and I'm giving back to others now. It's contagious. You ought to try it yourself. It's a lot of fun." If the individual is really curious, I give him or her one of those cards with the church's phone number on it. (By the way, in case you are thinking of printing up your own cards, I should mention that I rarely get phone calls—hardly ever, in fact. Don't worry—you won't be overwhelmed.)

The point is that when I do these giveaways, I demonstrate the kindness of God to someone else. There is nothing mystical about this kindness—God is being kind to someone through me and that person goes away with a greater knowledge of God's love.

Generosity, Tithing and Giving

I have believed in the principle of tithing for decades now. Since the beginning of our marriage, Janie and I have always given away 10 percent of our gross income to other people or to organizations we believe in. This principle has brought untold positive spins upon our finances and has kept us afloat during tough financial times. It is amazing how 90 percent of your gross income will take you further than 100 percent of it—even though it's unexplainable by modern math!

Janie and I also give money above and beyond this 10 percent through what we call "offerings." We put another 2 to 3 percent of our income into a fund that we can give away to friends who are in emergencies or to causes that we believe are worthy of a one-time gift from us. Our hearts beat fast for certain projects that we particularly like to support, such as the launchings of new churches. Perhaps your heart beats in the same way for special projects or certain kinds of people who struggle in life, but you don't feel that you can afford to support them.

We have found that there's no easy way to begin tithing (that is, giving 10 percent of your income to good causes beyond yourself). We encourage people to just jump in with both feet. Over the past 25 years, Janie and I have challenged hundreds and hundreds of people to begin tithing. I have personally offered to pay people back after 90 days for the money they have tithed if they weren't convinced that it was a worthwhile thing to do. Believe it or not, in all of those 25 years not a single person has ever come back to me and said that he or she thought it was a bad idea to tithe! When I think about it, this number must include well into the thousands of tithers. To me, this is proof positive that tithing is a rich, rewarding and fail-proof discipline.

Almost every book on personal finances encourages readers to give regularly—it's in both the spiritual and plain ol' motivational books alike. I take this a step further and say that we should give the *first* 10 percent of our income right off the top. I say this because I have found that if we wait until we get to our last 10 percent, we won't be able to afford to tithe. I've discovered this from experience. Tithing has to be our first priority.

Besides, tithing is just plain healthy. Focusing outward when it comes to our finances makes plenty of sense. When we catch the bug on this principle and invite God into our bank accounts and portfolios, our financial lives become very exciting. It's like going fishing with the guarantee of getting a catch. It's just a matter of what species of fish we will catch, how many we will catch and how big they will be.

Kindness Helps in Every Way

I think the most profound verse in the entire Bible is found in Romans 2:4, which basically states, "Don't you know that the kindness of God leads to repentance!" This is just amazing to me.

For years, I had read that verse and assumed that the "kindness of God" referred to something that was vertical—that it came down in some sort of revelation from God. I thought that maybe we would be driving down the freeway one day and a light would go on in our hearts that would make us realize that God was kind. Or that maybe we would be praying and suddenly experience the revelation that God was kind, which would then draw us to Him. Or even perhaps that we would hear an inspiring message from someone like Billy Graham and suddenly comprehend that God is kind. However, I now realize that none of these ideas are what God means when He says that He is kind. I believe that God is very practical. When one person is kind to another person in the name of God, this is God showing His kindness.

This realization came about when someone showed kindness to me by washing my car for free as a demonstration of God's love. It was the first and only time the person has ever done this, but it had a big impact on me. I realized that day that kindness is horizontal—it goes from one person to another. When one person shows kindness to another person, God shows up. The Bible says that when this happens, we desire to repent. The word "repent" may sound a little scary, but actually it just means that we desire to change our ways and become more like God. In short, it means that we desire to become like Jesus. Who among us doesn't want to become more like Him?

These days, Christianity is controversial not only in the United States but also across the world. There are many opinions about the Church. I have lived outside of the United States and gained an understanding of how outsiders view Christianity. I also read and watch the news a great deal—I'm a bona fide news junkie, in fact. One thing that I find interesting based on all of these inputs is that while the followers of Jesus are often controversial, basically everyone across the world respects the person of Jesus. Even the radical followers of Islam who hate Christianity don't hate Jesus. They honor Him. Strong critics of the Church have little if any negative statements to make about Christ. He is universally loved, or at least looked up to by the majority of people in the world.

Perhaps the Doobie Brothers said it best in their song from the 1970s: "Jesus Is Just Alright with Me." (Of course, He is way beyond being "just alright," but that's a good starting point.) The Bible tells us that Jesus went about *doing good to everyone He met*. He was habitually doing good things for the people He met in His travels. He was kindness embodied. He was a walking and talking force for good on Earth. Have you met people who have been Jesus to you? I met a few during the course of my recovery.

Play It Again, Harry

One of the people who demonstrated kindness to me was the ICU nurse at the first hospital. She cared in ways that no one else did. She thought from my perspective.

While I was still paralyzed and in a light coma, someone—God bless 'em—thought I would enjoy listening to the Harry Connick Jr. Christmas album. I guess he or she thought that the music would lift my spirit. The album was played and played and played and played and played . . . over and over and over again. It must have been played at least 100 times. I really like Harry Connick Jr.'s music, but not *that* much!

The ICU nurse figured out one day that I wasn't able to tell anyone I was going a little crazy listening to the album, so she actually hid the CD player and put on some non-Christmas music (*thank God!*). That small act of kindness meant the world to me. No one else took the time to recognize the world from my perspective.

The nurse did other things to show kindness to me, such as brushing my teeth—even though I smelled like rotting flesh! It didn't matter to her; she just dove right in. I'm sure that she could have gotten out of the job if she wanted to. I later remember that she was very curious about Jesus. She had dozens of questions to ask me about Him, and I answered as many as I had the energy to respond to.

Experiencing these acts of kindness from the ICU nurse reminded me of another act of kindness that I was shown back in high school. The experience turned out to be an important turning point in my young life. I went to a rock concert in Phoenix to see Alice Cooper. Now, if you are under 30 years old, you probably don't even know who Alice Cooper is. Suffice it to say, Alice is a *guy* who was a very popular shock rocker once upon a time back in the 1970s and early 1980s.

As I left the concert with my ears ringing from the volume of the loudspeakers, I ran into a group of bona fide Jesus Freaks in the parking lot. They had a VW van that was painted with bright colors and had unusual flowers and designs on it. There were Bible verses painted on the van as well. These Jesus Freaks were giving away comic books that had a Christian message. They weren't asking for donations—the comic books were completely free.

I remember being impressed that these people looked a lot like me—they had long hair just like me. However, the way they smiled seemed to indicate that they had something on the inside that I didn't have. This intrigued me. I don't remember what the comic book was about, but I certainly remember the fact that these people offered a free gift to me. I could tell these Christians weren't into it for the money. They just really loved people.

I stopped to talk to them for a moment and found that they seemed willing to talk as long as I wanted to talk. Of course, I didn't really want to talk—I was just testing them to see if they were for real. I felt the kindness of God in a strong way through their free gift. (Sometimes I wonder if they met Alice Cooper and gave him a comic book. He now believes very similarly to what they believed.)

The Healing Power of Kindness

Kindness is the greatest healing force in the world. It is the active form of love that is loosed upon people's lives. When we are kind, it turns us in the right direction and causes us to think differently. Kindness is contagious.

Janie and I have been coaching a church in a suburb of Copenhagen, Denmark, for the past few years. This growing fellowship uses active kindness as their primary means for outreach to the city. By touching people in the city through their simple acts of kindness, this congregation has been successful in gaining the attention of many people who don't normally want to have anything to do with the Church.

One young guy who they reached out to is named Peter. During one of their outreach ventures, the people in the church went from door to door handing out lightbulbs. When they knocked on Peter's door, the young man was sitting on his couch contemplating suicide—he was thinking about taking his own life that very day! He was depressed over the breakup of his relationship to a girl whom he had been dating for many years. He needed healing in his life.

Peter's story is typical of many people in Denmark. He had been away from the Church ever since he was a small child. He had tried organized religion, but found that it offered him nothing that was real and authentic. But his opinion of the Church changed that day when this small band of hearty souls arrived at his doorstep and offered him a gift of kindness.

A couple of months later, Peter was walking along the sidewalk in the city center when these carriers of kindness approached him and gave him a bottle of water. By this time, they had Peter's undivided attention. He was so curious about these individuals that he came to their Saturday night gathering at a coffee house. He enjoyed himself thoroughly.

Peter's first visit to the church took place over a year ago. Since that time, he has become connected with God in a very personal way. He has become a carrier of kindness himself and is now one of the most prolific practitioners of kindness in town. Peter experienced the healing power that the kindness of God brings. Now, giving away God's kindness is the driving force in his life.

The Tale of Two Bumper Stickers

I saw a bumper sticker the other day that simply read "Choose Life." I suspect that this message could be taken many different ways, but I took it to mean that we should believe the best about others. In other words, we should choose to believe life and not death about people when the option is given to us.

Everybody is either a life-giving person or a life-taking person. Our bodies give off signals, our words give off signals, our emotions give off signals, and our eyes are especially powerful at giving off life-giving or life-taking signals. There seems to be no middle ground. We are either draining people or encouraging them. We are either building up our neighbors or tearing them down.

This is why thinking the best about people is so vital. One line from 1 Corinthians 13 (referred to as the "love chapter") often read at weddings is the phrase "Love believes the best." Love chooses to believe the best about others no matter the circumstances. When we *choose* to believe the best in others, we show them love and actively demonstrate the life-giving kindness of God.

In the 1980s, the Random Acts of Kindness movement got started in various places around the United States. Across the land, bumper stickers that proclaimed "practice random acts of kindness and senseless acts of beauty" started to pop up. The bumper sticker was in response to the unexplainable acts of violence that were escalating in major cities across the United States.

At nearly the same time, I started what I dubbed "servant outreach" in Cincinnati. I was leading teams throughout this not-so-friendly city doing acts of kindness and generosity toward complete strangers. Our job, as we put it, was to make neighbors out of strangers and friends out of mere acquaintances through acts of generosity in our city of two million people. We were out to serve our way into the heart of the city.

Both movements developed independently. Both movements produced books and gained notoriety. My first book, *Conspiracy of Kindness*, has sold over 120,000 copies in its first 10 years of publication. It has been translated into six languages, with more translations in the works.

Dancing at the Waffle House

In the end, our reputation is all that we have that counts. It's what precedes us in life and it's what we leave behind when we are gone from the scene. We need to be the kind of people whom others weep about losing when we are gone from the picture. We need to aspire to be missed that much when we leave a job or move from a city. I truly am committed to the power of kindness to change the world, whether it be one jukebox song at a time, one donut at a time, or one dance at a time. Let me explain.

Each year on Christmas Eve, we have a tradition in our church of visiting people who have to work on that very important family night. Last Christmas Eve, we went to 500 locations around the city, including fire stations, EMT stations, police stations, gas stations, hotels, motels, restaurants, Alco centers and hospitals.

We first break into groups of 5 to 10 people (usually one of our small groups). When the groups arrive at their designated locations, they give the workers a fresh box of donuts, sing a Christmas carol and offer to pray for them. The carol is often turned down, but the prayer rarely is!

During one of these Christmas Eve visitations, a group went to a local restaurant called the Waffle House to deliver their donuts. The group's plan of attack was simple: Half the group would wash dishes in the back of the restaurant to give the dishwasher a break while the other half would proceed to the front to see if they could get diners to dance with them. I guess the group figured that many of the patrons would be rather depressed—which was a good assumption in my mind, considering it was Christmas Eve and the diners were alone.

The washing crew washed dishes for the better part of an hour and had a blast. The dishwasher was thrilled to get the help. He said that it was his Christmas present! The crew up front, meanwhile, began inserting dollar bills into the jukebox and playing upbeat and antidepressing songs. They primarily picked out Motown songs, which are great for getting people up and moving in the right direction emotionally.

As the group played the songs, they started pulling people out of their booths and tables to dance. People were reluctant at first, but eventually most of them got up and began to dance. That's a real feat in Cincinnati! Soon the entire restaurant was up and dancing. No kidding—all of the people in the Waffle House were dancing!

As the small group left, all the people shouted in one accord, "See you next year, all you Vineyard people!" The group didn't realize that they had agreed to come back next year!

A week later, I received a call from a psychologist. He said that he had two patients who didn't know one another but happened to be at the Waffle House that night. The two ended up dancing together.

"I'm sorry we made them dance!" I said, assuming the worst.

"No, it was wonderful," the psychologist replied. "Normally they are terribly depressed during this time of the year, but it looks like this year they are doing pretty good—way better than normal. I'm cutting back on their medication, in fact." There was a slight pause after this.

"I just have one question for you," the psychologist said after a moment. "Do you normally dance to the tunes of Diana Ross on Sunday mornings at your church?"

I'm a pretty practical guy, so all I could think to say was, "Well, not yet!"

CHAPTER 11

DYING TO BE A BETTER NEIGHBOR

Cincinnati circa 1985 was best known for its chili, its one-time mayor Jerry Springer, and a silly sitcom about a radio station and a dumb blonde. Besides the baseball-playing Big Red Machine, there wasn't much for the warblers to chirp about. Cincinnati needed a new vibe.

It was in 1985 that a small crowd of city dignitaries and local artisans gathered at Columbia Plaza (now Chiquita Plaza) on East Fifth Street to dedicate an 18-foot-tall colorful piece of public art titled "The Cincinnati Story." George Sugarman created the metal mass of 16 cutouts that spring forth from a reflecting pool. The idea was to depict the city of Cincinnati emerging from the Ohio River in all its vibrancy. It was a good sentiment.

Also in 1985, just two blocks west at Fountain Square, the people of Chabad and Congregation Lubavitch erected a menorah and displayed it during Hanukkah. Fountain Square is the symbolic heart of Cincinnati, and the menorah's presence became a warm holiday tradition—another positive sign that the community was re-emerging. The year 1985 also marked the arrival of Larry Bonhaus. He joined the Cincinnati Civic Orchestra as its conductor. The orchestra now performs in concert halls, parks and churches throughout the region. Now the city had music!

Okay, these benchmarks by themselves do not mean much, but they were small indicators that Cincinnati, despite its reputation for snobbery, still had a latent community spirit. When Janie and I arrived in town that same year, we set out to find it. We decided to intentionally put the word "community" right in the name of our new church.

The Intentional Neighbor

Unless you live on a ranch in the middle of Wyoming, you probably have neighbors. Even if this were the case, you would still have to interact with people in your community at some time. It is called the human condition.

Given the fact that relating to others is unavoidable, you can thus choose just how neighborly you want to be. Long ago, Janie and I decided that we wanted to be intentionally neighborly, and we have found many ways to go about doing this.

I am a big coffee drinker. I end up winning people over to drinking coffee wherever I go. If they didn't like coffee before they met me, they almost always end up connoisseurs afterward. I even like chewing espresso beans! I find that there are two ways to drink coffee: standing up or sitting down. There are two temperatures at which coffee can be served: hot or cold. It is a great social drink. When I offer someone a cup of joe, I am being a good neighbor. When java is served, my friendship antennae go up and activate. I gab. I laugh. I cry. I listen. I pour a second cup.

If coffee doesn't work, a soak in a hot tub may. Janie and I installed a nice hot tub a few years ago as a way to intentionally connect with our neighbors. We had it sunk into our new deck so that I could easily step into it. There is something universally appealing about hot water, relaxing jets and soothing music. It often causes people to open up to heart-to-heart conversation.

We bought our current house specifically because it had a swimming pool. We thought that it would be a magnet for gathering friends and neighbors. Sure enough, the pool has made our house a mini YMCA. It's packed every day in the summer.

We do not simply expect people to come to us. Janie and I take walks in the morning and in the evening with our tiny dogs—a couple of Yorkshire Terriers. Our dogs' faces look a lot like the Ewoks from *Star Wars*. Dogs are natural attractants. They cause people to pause and open up to you. People will often stop what they are doing and strike up a conversation with us—or at least with our Yorkies.

Right now we have some special neighbors who live across the street. Although we don't have the dog factor in common, we discovered that both we and our neighbors used to live in California. They moved in last year, and we really enjoy spending time with one another. We invite our new neighbors over to our home to watch movies. They often host parties to sell products to those who attend, so every few months Janie and I attend a different product party to support their latest venture. We always buy a thing or two to encourage them. By the way, are you looking for a complete set of cinnamon-scented candles? I'm thinking of selling my latest purchase on e-bay.

Before my injury, I wouldn't have had the time to go to parties such as these. I would have considered them a waste of time. And I definitely wouldn't have bought anything. This kind of marketing just wasn't my thing. But I have changed. I now realize that I need to invest in relationships in order to be a good neighbor. I understand that it's necessary to encourage our neighbors when they are hosting a party, for example. If it's important to them, it ought to be at least a little important to me because I'm their neighbor. I really don't need any other reason. If they had children who took piano lessons, I would be eager to go to their recitals, even if the children couldn't play chopsticks very well.

Another way that Janie and I decided to reach out to our neighbors was to put a big-time video theater into our basement. We saved for a long time to be able to get this. Sure, it's an excuse to have a party and show cool DVDs, but a big part of our motivation was to have a place to entertain our neighbors. And it has worked! We have people over constantly.

Since I died and came back to life, friendships with my neighbors have become far more important to me. I think back to some of the great neighbors that our family has had over the years. One particular family stands out. They were great neighbors because they were available to us. They were kind to our son, Jack. We would take turns watching one another's children. They had a way of anticipating our needs, and we tried to do the same for them. They were there for us and we were there for them.

One thing that was kind of irritating (and humorous at the same time) about these neighbors was that they were always trying to convert us to their faith. They were Midwest hardcore biker Mormons! Having lived in the western part of the United States, I've discovered that the most dedicated Mormons don't live in Utah and Arizona—they live in places like Ohio, Indiana and Missouri.

I respect Mormons—I have many relatives who are Mormons. I explained to these neighbors that I was the pastor of a church, but that didn't seem to slow them down one bit—they were excited about their cause. Although years have come and gone since our families moved away, we still keep in regular contact. In fact, we just received a letter from these former neighbors with a recent photo of their children. Good neighbors do that sort of thing over the years. I just wish that I had been a bit more intentional about it.

Leaving the Cocoon

Good neighbors are hard to come by these days—or maybe it's just that they hardly ever come by at all! When was the last time you said hello to the people who live two houses down the street? Do you even know your neighbors' names?

We all are so dug in these days. Author and futurist Faith Popcorn calls this condition "cocooning." We tend to stay to ourselves in our castles—uh, I mean our homes in the suburbs. We don't like to be disturbed. And we're usually too tired to socialize.

In the days of my grandparents before the advent of air conditioning, people used to sit outside to cool off and socialize. Today, most people don't even have a front porch. People now just tend to keep to themselves, unless an airplane crashes in the neighborhood or some other disaster occurs.

Janie and I use events on the calendar as an excuse to get people in our neighborhood together to just hang out. For example, each Halloween in our cul-de-sac we build a big fire in our portable fire pit, place it at the end of our driveway, and then bring out all the makings for s'mores. We are kind of off the beaten path for trick-or-treaters, so we typically don't get too many kids that come out for candy. But the adults sure have a great time hanging out and just gabbing for several hours. In today's world, we have to create reasons to get together. We must consciously plan to spend time together with our neighbors, or we will never get to know them.

We all need to be people persons deep down, all the time. We need to develop skills that put us in touch with those around us in an individual way. Jesus continually spoke of the importance of being a good neighbor and modeled for us what being a good neighbor is all about. He was warm toward everyone. He remembered people's names. When Jesus met people, He not only spoke profound words that brought encouragement to them—words they never forgot for the rest of their lives—but He also did things for them. Jesus and the disciples (better known as "the Twelve") continually demonstrated hospitality to those around them. They bought food for the needy and provided meals for thousands on several occasions. Of course, some of these acts of hospitality were also miracles, but we should not forget that these were also acts of hospitality that displayed the awesome power of God.

The Ten Commandments are roughly divided up into two sections—the part that has to do with how we treat God and the part that has to do with how we treat our friends and neighbors. The people who opposed Jesus focused completely on the parts of the Commandments that dealt with how they were to treat God. They had no concern with how they were supposed to treat their neighbors. But Jesus came along and said that was only part of the story. He told these people that if they didn't treat their neighbors in the right way, they were blowing it completely.[1] He applied the truth of God to life—He didn't live it out in a vacuum.

After my accident, I was called by God to remember those commands that Jesus put so much weight on—the people-centered commands. Prior to my accident, it was so easy for me to get caught up in the things of life and simply forget about the priority of fellowshipping with others. It was easy to forget that people are what it's really all about. But to forget this is to ultimately blow it in the end—even if we are living our lives with excellence and resourcefulness and are going mostly in the right direction.

Jesus promises that He will judge us when all is said and done. He will judge us based on our works and the motivation behind those works. He promises that He will judge all of us—

sinners and saints alike.[2] This means that even those people who seem to have done all the right things outwardly could fail the Jesus litmus test miserably.

We all know that it's possible to do things that appear to be right but have the wrong motives. Not long ago, I was downtown and ran into someone whom I call "bullhorn guy." As I approached him, I heard him cry the words "sin," "Jesus" and "hell," followed by threats that we all better respond to his message or we might die tonight. No one was listening to bullhorn guy. No one was taking his literature. He was not being a good neighbor. Quite the contrary—he was being a bad neighbor. He was trying to shock people into coming to God's love, but in reality he was just pushing them away.

As I watched bullhorn guy shout at the passersby, I wondered if he had read his Bible. The Bible clearly says that if we say we love God, whom we have never seen, we must also love our fellow man, whom we see around us each and every day.[3] It seems that the lack of understanding of this verse is at the very core of why so many religious people push others away from God. Unfortunately, even though I didn't have a bullhorn, in my own way I was doing my fair share of pushing.

We don't have to be as in-your-face as bullhorn guy to be a stumbling block to others. We can have all the right motives but actually block people from seeing the love of Jesus.

The New Cincinnati Kids

Friendliness begets friendliness. Treat others the way you want to be treated. As you demonstrate kindness, that kindness will come back to you and affect entire communities. Wow, I am full of pithy maxims today. Good thing they work!

I have seen the evidence of friendship in action on both a personal level and in my community. For 20 years, the people of the Vineyard Community Church and other churches have shown kindness to the city of Cincinnati. During this time, the city has changed in measurable ways. Before we started doing large-scale events to show love, kindness and mercy to the community (such as handing out bottles of water to people on a hot day or cleaning toilets), the people of Cincinnati were widely known as standoffish. It was not easy to make friends with people—the joke was that "the new kid on the block has been here for 10 years." It got so bad that there were even race riots.

Today, there is a new vibe in the city. In 2004, a group called the Partners for Livable Communities chose Cincinnati as one of the 10 most livable cities in America. There was even a big award ceremony. *Esquire* magazine, in its top 10 list, simply stated that Cincinnati rocks.

People seek this place out because it has a fresh atmosphere. It is hard to describe, but it is noticeable. We have new vibes! What made the difference? Certainly, many things changed this town that I have come to call home. But one thing I know for sure is that God used the Vineyard Community Church, other area churches and thousands of individual Christians as spark plugs to ignite change. We were good neighbors. And now, our community *rocks*.

Notes
1. See Mark 12:31,38-40.
2. See Matthew 19:28-30.
3. See 1 John 4:20.

CHAPTER 12

DYING TO KNOW WHAT TO SAY

When I was in the hospital and it looked as if I was not going to make it, quite a few people visited me and made feeble attempts to bring closure with me. Almost no one said anything to me that made sense or brought me comfort. Most of the men gave me a pep talk similar to the one a coach would give during halftime in the locker room when his team was getting clobbered. These pep talks usually went something like this: "You can make it! Let's get out there and kick their behinds and win, win, win!" The women usually cried and said very little. That made me sad.

One person who did make sense was an older lady who came to visit me. She said something like this:

> I will never be the same again after you are gone, for you have touched me in a way that has permanently changed my life. I can never go back

to living the way I lived before I met you. You have touched me in a deep, profound and permanent way. Know that when you are gone, part of me will go with you. Thank you.

She then kissed my hand and left. The more that I have reflected on what this older lady said, the more I have realized that this was about the only thing one could say to a friend who is dying. If a person has truly shared his or her life, we will never be the same once that person is gone. Saying much of anything else is surface clutter—some of which is silly.

The friendship that can cease has never been real.

—Saint Jerome

What in the Middle Ages was known as the ars morendi, *the "art of dying," is something for which our society has not developed any sort of cultural background.*

—Hans Kung

A Plan for the End

My accident instantly ushered me into a new season of life. My body went through permanent changes, as did my emotions. I went hurling into an unknown future, whether I liked it or not.

Everybody passes through different seasons in life. From the moment we are born we are in transition. The 1960s rock band the Byrds sang, "To everything—turn, turn, turn—there is a season . . . a time to be born, and a time to die." [1] They were speaking a profound truth about life that is inescapable for each of us—eventually, at some unknown moment in the future, we will all die.

Death is unavoidable, and yet most of us are not prepared. Funeral homes market themselves on the idea that we must make the necessary physical arrangements for our burial long before we breathe our last. They even make a point that when death comes, those left behind have other emotions to sort through and should not have to worry about the details of a memorial service. Such preparations are unpleasant for most of us, but they really shouldn't be. If we have done our business with God, we have nothing to fear.

When it comes time to die, make sure all you have to do is die.
—Jim Elliot

Far more often than just thinking through our own demise, we will have to face the prospect of losing our friends and loved ones. When this occurs, we need to know how to approach these individuals with love, gentleness and grace. We need to think through these situations in advance. Having gone through this experience, I can tell you that most people don't have a clue what to say when someone close to them is dying.

As I was writing this chapter, I received a phone call from a friend. He is currently facing a serious operation and is nervous about the outcome. There is a chance that he won't survive the surgical procedure. I am going to stop by later today to visit him and give him some assurance. I hope to undo some of the damage that others have unwittingly done in their attempts to say something meaningful to him—people who didn't know what to say but tried to give him pep talks, or who just cried. My friend has already done his business with God, so he has the ultimate answer to his fears. At worst, he is a little nervous. He hasn't had much time to get used to the idea of what he is facing. After all, he's only 39 years old.

I hope that I say the right things.

How to Approach Someone Who Is Dying

Having visited many people who were dying (and having gone through it myself), I've discovered a handful of timeless principles that will help you be a friend to someone who is dying. Of course, we're not talking about deep counseling here—these are just some practical things that you can do and say to communicate you care for the person without leaving him or her feeling down. Here are some of these principles.

- **Don't be overly somber.** This is probably the most important point to remember. Don't cry. People who are near death have already been struggling and crying, especially if their terminal illness came on suddenly. The last thing they need is for someone to bring them down further. Put away the shovel so you don't dig a deeper hole for them. They need someone to bring them up. A cheerful attitude is good medicine.
- **Don't tell the dying person that he or she is dying.** This is not your job. Leave it to the doctors or the person's close family. Besides, you don't even know for sure if the person is going to die. God has the final word on all things regarding life and death.
- **Be positive and upbeat.** Smile when you talk to the person. If it seems appropriate, kid with him or her a bit. I'm a teaser, so I naturally rag people most of the time regardless of the circumstances. People know that and expect it from me. If I didn't behave that way, they would think something was wrong with me!
- **If appropriate, bring the person the gift of music.** The environment of a hospital room can be very bor-

ing and depressing. Bring in a CD that is uplifting and soothing. Such music is great for the heart. Perhaps you have an iPod with lots of songs on it that the person can choose from. If the person doesn't have a boombox to play a CD on, you can loan yours to him or her. (Of course, it would be most helpful if the player you loaned had a remote control feature.)

- **Consider bringing the Bible on CD.** It is powerful to listen to the words of Scripture. Listening to a modern and easy-to-understand translation such as the *New Living Bible*, the *New International Version* or *THE MESSAGE* can be very encouraging to the individual. You will end up investing around $100 for a set of CDs covering the entire Bible, but it is worth the cost.

If you are a spiritual person, your dying friend may want to talk with you about things of a spiritual nature. He or she may want to get your opinion on heaven. If you feel that you have a mooring and can be honest and provide some hope, go ahead and talk about eternity. Depending on where your friend is spiritually, he or she is probably looking for answers. No one wants to face death without hope.

As a well-spent day brings happy sleep, so life well used brings happy death.

—Leonardo da Vinci

I was free from fears during my medical accident because I had figured out my eternal destiny. We owe it to ourselves to settle the issue of death and dying between us and God. We can't live our lives strongly until we have settled the issue once and for all.

When it comes to approaching a dying person, we can never know the perfect things to say. But we can bring hope into a person's situation that will add quality to his or her last days.

Note
1. The Byrds, "Turn, Turn, Turn (There Is a Season)," *Turn, Turn, Turn,* Sony Music Company, copyright 1965. Original lyrics by Pete Seeger.

CHAPTER 13

DYING TO LIVE TO 90

Okay, I admit it. I am not ready to die again—not yet. I have too much living to do. Doctors (we have a love-hate relationship) warn me that my internal organs took a toll and may not last the usual 77.3 years. Of course, I know that we all have that unknown moment in our future when we must pass on. But I am not buying into the doctor's prognosis. I will die again, but I do not plan on doing so until I am well into my 90s. Don't believe me? Ah, then you have never read my journals.

My Journal and My Prayers

I write in my journal every day—have done so for years. I started out with a traditional journal, but today I use journaling software on my Macintosh laptop (I know, how high-tech of me!). I reflect, record events, write down dreams and scribble down random thoughts. I force myself to be transparent. My journal has been a great tool for my personal growth, both emotionally and spiritually. It has also helped me to set goals and keep them. Let me explain.

I read every motivational book I can get my hands on—have for years. Most motivational books encourage people to write out goals and stick to them. I started keeping a record of my goals when I was 14. Every day I would write out my short-term and long-term objectives. In essence, I would set up targets. As I aimed for my goals, my grades went from a few Bs and mostly Cs to all As for the rest of my high school career and throughout my college career. I got incredible jobs that paid very well. And I met and married the woman of my dreams.

Write and Pray

For many years, I tried to pray as most people do—by just talking with God. I would kneel, close my eyes, open my eyes, recite the Lord's prayer, talk casually—I tried all of the approaches. I really did try, but none of these methods seemed to work with consistency. Of course, there were moments when I felt a connection with God and experienced the excitement of answered prayers, but there were lots of yawns and wandering thoughts, too.

I now write out many of my prayers in my journal. I find this to be a helpful way to pray and keep my mind focused. A few years after I began doing this, I discovered that many leaders over the centuries also took this approach. It feels good to know that I'm not the only person who at times finds it a challenge to pray!

As I pray and write, I include my goals—both short-term (those that I'm working on for that day or week) and long-term (those that will take years to come about). I keep things manageable by limiting my list to just 10 goals in either category. In my experience, I have found that if I have more than 10 goals in the short-term or long-term category, I am typically too busy to complete them all and I grow frustrated. If I start to see my schedule push up past 10 goals in either category, I start working on simplifying my life. I begin saying no to opportunities that come my way so that I can focus on my priorities.

My list of goals is different than my to-do list. I limit my goals to 10 items, but I might have a to-do list for each goal that includes many more tasks. For example, a goal would be to complete this book (and I think that this will be the last chapter, even though it is hard to know exactly where to stop when your life's story goes on), so my to-do list might contain 10 things that I have to do to accomplish that goal. I might have to set up a website, approve the cover design, thank Todd Hunter for writing the foreword, and approve a change that my editor wants to make. Each of these are to-do list tasks that enable me to reach my final goal of completing this book.

I might also have to-do items that are not directly related to goals. For instance, I might have lunch with my daughter Laura, buy a birthday present for Janie, or have the snow shoveled out of the driveway. Some of these will be related to life-long goals, some will not.

The Power of Goals

Goals are incredibly powerful. They exert power over our lives and affect how we think, act and feel. Goals can change the course of our personal histories. When enough people work together toward accomplishing the same goal, the history of a city—or even of an entire nation—can be changed.

During World War II, cities and towns in the United Kingdom were bombed by the Nazi forces on an almost daily basis. At the peak of the attacks, it was widely anticipated that Churchill would announce that England would capitulate. But instead, Churchill gave his most rousing speech. It lasted all of 20 seconds. Churchill simply walked into the pressroom, puffed his cigar and said, "Never, never, never, never give up. That's it, boys!"

The utter resolve and simplicity of that speech captured the hearts and minds of the people of England. The British fought on. Although they suffered severe civilian casualties, they realized that they were on the same page and shared a common goal. Churchill had the gift of putting courage into powerful words. His goal became the people's goal. Imagine how different history would have been if Churchill had decided that his nation needed to cut its losses and run.

In the same way, the goals that we set for our life and our family will change our personal history. When it came to the woman that I would marry, I set goals and prayed. Let me explain.

Long before I met Janie, I asked God to give me a wife. But not just any wife—I wrote down in my journal specific attributes about the kind of mate that I wanted. Sometime when you have moment, find a Bible that is easy to read and look up Proverbs 31. (Proverbs is almost at the center of the Bible.) That chapter in Proverbs describes the kind of woman I sought. It paints a picture of a woman who is entrepreneurial and works with her hands with delight. She rises early to care for her family; in other words, she isn't afraid of hard work.

When other people look at the man who is married to such a woman, they call him fulfilled. This is a man who has married above himself! If you ever meet Janie, you will definitely agree that I married up. In fact, I usually explain that when I married Janie, I not only married up—I married above my species! I often tell people that they will like me more once they have met her. Most of our friends will agree.

Before I met Janie, I dated lots of women. Some of them were wealthy. Many of them were beautiful and had great personalities. But none of them were like the woman I had described in my journal. Not one of these women represented the gift that I knew was coming my way. I wrote about Janie in my journal and waited for about 10 years until she finally appeared on the scene.

Today, Janie and I set goals together (Janie keeps a journal as well). We believe that we will both live long lives and work actively well into our 80s. This is not because of economic reasons—Janie and I have invested well and we could afford to retire sooner. But we couldn't imagine not working. We love to be active. We love to work hard. We both love to mentor others and envision pouring ourselves into younger leaders for the rest of our lives. Picture two 80-somethings hanging around with lots of 20-somethings—you get the idea.

So how does this affect our goal setting? Janie and I talk regularly about what life will be like several decades from now. We are currently building a house in Tampa and are making plans to move there. We envision ourselves mentoring people, writing books and speaking at seminars. While we both believe that we will work into our 80s, we also feel strongly that we will live into our mid-90s. God has given us an expectation that we will live and live well.

Write, Pray and *Listen*

I was at home one day on a Saturday afternoon. Now, I should mention that I usually don't shave on Saturdays. In fact, if I'm not out of town on a speaking engagement, sometimes I don't even shower. I *really* take the day off! That particular Saturday, I hadn't showered and I looked pretty grubby. My hair was sticking straight up (Janie loves me no matter what I look like as long as I brush my teeth!).

It was mid-afternoon. As I was writing in my journal and praying, I suddenly had a thought: *Pray hard for Carole Cochrane.* Carole had just turned 72 and was a good friend of ours. She had developed a severe case of pneumonia in both her lungs and was not expected to live. Dana, her daughter, had been called to the hospital "for the last time" on several occasions—that's how close Carole was to succumbing to the illness.

As I prayed, I had an inspired thought: *Go down to the hospital right now—don't delay. I'll tell you what to say when you get there.* Now, this sort of thinking doesn't often leap into my mind, so I was hesitant. However, the "I'll tell you" part in the thought indicated to me that it was probably God who was doing the inspiring. So I thought it through and finally reasoned, *I really love Carole and I've got nothing to lose. She's desperate.* I saved my journal file, switched off my computer and headed to the hospital.

When I arrived, the nurses in the critical care unit were a little reluctant to let me in. I had put on a baseball cap so that my hair would look a little less scary, but I guess I still didn't look too sanitary! Finally, I convinced the nurses that a visit from me would not hurt.

In my years of caring for sick people, I don't think I've ever seen someone who looked as bad as Carole did that day. The first thing she said was, "I've been praying that I will die. I'm just miserable."

What could I say to that? Not even my own advice on encouraging people close to death could redeem that kind of resolve. However, it was a day for inspired thoughts, and at that moment I had another one.

"Carole," I said, "I've got some good news and some bad news for you. The bad news is that you are going to die." Carole looked a little downcast at that remark, but not surprised.

"What's the good news?" she asked.

"The good news is that you aren't going to die for another 20 years!" At that, Carole's face lit up. I asked if I could pray for her, and she said, "Gladly!" I prayed very briefly, asking God to lift the virus off of Carole and bring her back to 100 percent health. After the prayer, I said, "Take care," and left.

Dana called me a couple of days later. "I don't know what happened when you prayed," she said, "but it was dramatic. My mother is completely free from all traces of the pneumonia—in just two days! The doctors are stunned. She's home now."

It sounded religious, but I said it anyway: "Amen!"

The point of the story is that I don't think I would have received the inspired thought to pray for Carole if I hadn't been journaling and writing out my prayers. I know myself well enough to realize that I just don't hear spiritual things like this during the daily flow of life. If I don't make it a point to slow down, my internal metronome ticks so fast as I go from one point to the next that I never hear anything—much less a message from God. If I hadn't adopted the practice of setting long-term goals as a way of thinking, I don't think that the thought of Carole living a certain number of years would have crossed my mind.

I've been around this practice of trying to hear the voice of God for a long time. It is definitely not an exact science. I have met a few people who are tuned in, and I have even heard from God a few times myself. On the other hand, I have also met some people who were trying so hard to be inspired by God that they did some pretty odd things.

Yet the apostle Paul said that we shouldn't despise people's efforts to get inspired thoughts. In his first letter to the Thessalonians, he said, "Don't put out the Spirit's fire by treating such inspiration with contempt."[1] I can see what Paul was saying. It is easy to throw the baby out with the bathwater. Think about this for minute. Look back over your life. Haven't there been times when you realized that you had heard or seen something that was inspired? Use some common sense. Where do you think that inspiration came from?

When I teach on this subject, I use an illustration of children asking for help to find lost objects that eventually turn up in the most unlikely of places. This illustration probably came to me as an inspired thought that was based upon an experience from my childhood. I remember that when I was about 10 years old, I received a bow and arrow set for my birthday—just a little one that wasn't too dangerous. One time, I shot my arrow off into the grassy field near our house and lost it in the grass. I looked and looked in the area where I thought it had landed, but it was just impossible to find. I figured that it was gone for good. Finally, I prayed and said, "God, if you listen to prayers, show me where to look."

I soon got an inspired idea of where to look for the arrow, but it was quite a ways away from where I was standing. It seemed to be a very unlikely place to find it, but I thought, *What do I have to lose?* I walked over to the area and ran my finger under the grass roots. Sure enough, there was my lost arrow! I was amazed and convinced that God had heard my prayer.

My Funeral

It may seem kind of morbid to ask, but how do you picture your memorial service? What sort of people will gather together to celebrate your life? Who are they? What sort of walks of life do they come from? What will they say about you and the way that you lived your life? Will they weep because you are gone? Will they mourn because your good deeds have come to an end?

As I mentioned, I have written in my journal that I will live to be 90 years old or more. But when I die, people from all different age groups will gather and come to my funeral. In fact, I will probably have more friends in their 20s and 30s than in my age group. That's always been the case—it certainly is the case today, even though I am in my 50s.

At my funeral, people will look at pictures that capture some of the fun times we shared over the years. The photos will depict places such as Los Angeles, Oslo, Baltimore, Cincinnati and Tampa—all the places where Janie and I planted churches. We're avid photographers, so there will be no shortage of photos.

Church planters will converge on Tampa for the memorial service. By that time, the number of churches that Janie and I have planted will number around 100, so there will be a lot of people who will want to share about their experiences of being coached and mentored by me. We'll have to keep the sharing to a minimum so that things don't get boring!

People from some of the churches will speak about the great relationships we shared over the years. They will share about how we were very generous toward one another financially. Other leaders in town will say that I am in a far better place now and that they envy me. Someone will say that I can finally stop writing books—and then everyone will laugh.

I will be cremated. My ashes will be spread in the Tampa Bay, where I loved to fish. A number of people will float out in a small armada to help spread the ashes and drink some Perrier water and lime in my honor as the sun goes down.

Solomon was the wisest man to ever walk the earth. He wrote the book of Proverbs from the perspective of one who had lived a full life and then reflected upon that life from the end to the beginning. He encourages us to live our lives from that same wise perspective. So live your life from the time of your funeral (your ultimate victory party!) to the present. Strategize things so that you will have a life that is thought out in clear ways.

A very small percentage of people have a written life plan that is complete with recorded goals for themselves. I believe the reason for this reluctance is fear of disappointment. We are fearful to dream because all the details of our plan might not come true. But we have to step out and risk dreaming just the same.

My Last Story

I love telling stories! (You noticed, eh?) Okay, well, this will be my last one in this book. I promise. It will be the last one because I am out of pages on which to write and because it makes a great concluding point for each of us—including me!

Just a couple of days ago, a local city leader that I had never met tracked me down. He was in tears when I picked up the phone. He said, "I have heard that you have had some success in praying for people who are sick. Is that true?"

"Sometimes people get better when I pray for them," I replied. "But I certainly can't control any of these sorts of things."

The man went on to talk about his dearly beloved mother who, at the age of just 62, recently found out that she has cancer all over her body. The doctors had told her that she had just a few months to live and had basically sent her home to die. (*Why do doctors do that?*) I agreed that I would visit his mother and pray for her.

As I walked into the woman's home, I immediately felt something positive. I recognized it as the presence of faith and knew that something was going to happen when we prayed. I sensed that I needed to tell the woman the story of my death and recovery (while I am not back to the shape that I was in before I died, I am much, much further along than most doctors thought I would be). As I told my story, the woman brightened up. I prayed for her and felt a strong sense of spiritual power upon her. She began to cry. She shook gently as the power of God came upon her.

When we had finished praying together, the woman and I agreed that it would be important for us to have more times of prayer, and I have since gone back on several occasions. But before I left that day, I told the woman about some of my impressions of death. "If you have a childlike relationship with God," I said, "you have nothing to fear in death. Death is not the big, scary, overwhelming enemy that our culture has made it out to be. Until we get past our fear of death, we will be prevented from taking risks in life."

There it is: three sentences that encapsulate what I learned the day I died. If you are reading this book and fear dying, reread what I said to this woman. You do not have to fear death. It really is that simple. There is a much better way to live.

I have more to say about death and life (yes, in that order), but I am at the end of my last chapter. I hope that doesn't sound like a cop-out. But I have a special website (dayidied.com) that clearly explains how you can overcome a persistent fear of death and live a life that will catapult you way beyond that nagging and persistent fear. I know that what I have to share on my website will bring liberation in your life. Please take a few minutes and check it out. You can also send me an e-mail at stevesjogren@mac.com. I love hearing from people and I respond to each e-mail that I receive—no kidding!

The best is yet to come! For Janie and me, the best means that we are moving on to Florida. But I will miss watching the squirrels play in the big tree with the hole in it in our backyard in Cincinnati.

Note
1. See 1 Thessalonians 5:20.

SINCE THE DAY I DIED

It has been a few years since the accident described in this book occurred. As I travel, people often ask me for updates. As of the time of the writing of this book, the following is how I typically respond.

How Do You Feel Now?

There are some aspects of my health that have improved significantly and some that just haven't changed much (and apparently won't change unless a miracle occurs). My quad muscles in my upper legs are basically all but gone. However, my doctors say that I am an interesting case—my legs have adapted to my situation wonderfully. Now my hamstrings (the muscles on the back of my legs) have become quite strong and do what my quads used to do.

I look pretty funny, though, when I'm wearing swimming trunks. My upper thighs look like birds' legs. I have lost all capacity to do things, such as rise out of a chair, without help. I can't do steps very well, especially when stepping down. I don't do ramps well, either. Anything other than a slow walk is beyond my capacity.

Frankly, this has been very depressing for me. Just when my son, Jack, was in need of a dad to play sports with him, I was taken out of commission. No basketball, no football, no Frisbee—and I used to be a magnificent Frisbee player! I can't even ride a bicycle. Most of all, I miss riding motorcycles—that was a big love of my life. I can no longer hold a bike up.

My legs tingle constantly—like pins and needles firing incessantly. Other than the tingling, I have no feeling in my legs. When doctors run tests on my legs, they stick long needles into my muscles and run an electrical current through the needles. I can't feel any of it.

I now take pain medication a couple of times a day. Without it, I wouldn't be able to tolerate the pain or to sleep at night.

How Are You Doing Emotionally After All of These Losses?

It has been very difficult to cope with all of the losses that I have been through and still come out smiling. I believe that I have become a much more authentic person and that I now have fewer (if any) filters. Everyone who knew me before the accident notices that I am a lot more deliberate than I was before.

The way I describe it is that before the accident, my internal metronome was ticking at 120 clicks per minute. I was always in a hurry to get from point *A* to point *B*. I rarely noticed things going on around me. Now my metronome is clicking away at about 25 clicks per minute.

At first, the clinical psychiatrists predicted that I would lose quite a few IQ points as a result of having an extremely low blood pressure for such a long time. But amazingly, the last two times that I took an IQ test, I scored 15 points and then 20 points higher than I have ever scored—even before the accident! I don't understand how this is possible, but that's what has happened.

To deal with my losses, I see a counselor on a regular basis. This connection has been invaluable in my life. I am a big fan of professional care. I like to say, "If you lost all that I lost through this experience, you'd be at least a little depressed too, I suspect." Some of my friends have been critical of me for seeing a professional counselor, but I don't care. I respectfully disagree with them. I believe that virtually all of us will need to see a counselor/psychologist/psychiatrist at some point in our lives. We may also need to take some medication for a time in order to get better.

Life is too short to drag around for months being ineffective and just gutting it out—some people that I've known have walked around in a state of depression for years and have been far less than effective in life. Life is far less difficult when we become honest with ourselves.

Physically, What Is Your Greatest Challenge Now?

Without a doubt, my greatest challenge (and frustration) is my loss of energy. I can only work so many hours a day and so many hours a week until I conk out. When I speak publicly and tell the story of the day I died, it takes me a day or two just to recover from that one speaking engagement.

Traveling overseas especially takes a toll on me. I used to speak 7 times on a weekend and was raring to go the next day. Literally overnight, all of that changed. I used to sleep 6 hours, maximum, and I was fine. Now I sleep 9 or 10 hours just to stay on top of things. I get a lot done with my time; I just have to be a lot more strategic with the hours that I have. Also, I have learned to work through teams to get things done!

Thanks to everyone for asking. If you are interested, I will post relevant updates on my website, dayidied.com.

THE DAY TERRI SCHIAVO DIED

The story of Terri Schiavo will forever be etched into all of our minds. The enormous press coverage of her death at a Tampa hospice in 2005 made sure of that fact.

I have quite a bit in common with Ms. Schiavo. As Terri Schiavo's story was being splashed across the front pages of the *New York Times* (the paper that I read each day), I couldn't help but notice numerous similarities between her case and mine. Maybe not in the specifics—her level of brain injury was completely different than mine—but there were numerous parts of our stories that were eerily similar.[1]

"He Is No Longer with Us . . ."

For starters, the night that my accident occurred, a team of doctors came to Janie and gave her counsel regarding my condition. They thought that I had sustained *significant brain damage* because my heart had stopped for a sustained period of time and I had been without significant blood pressure for such a long time (over an hour). They told my wife that this was definitely the case. But they didn't understand the power of many people praying together in unison.

Within minutes of my injury, a plea for people to pray for my healing went out on our church's popular website. News regarding my condition was updated on an hourly basis. There were thousands of names on the church's e-mail list, and each of these individuals were contacted and asked to pray. Within hours, literally tens of thousands of people across Europe, the United Kingdom, Asia, Canada and the United States—places where I had been speaking quite a bit over the past few years—were praying for God to intervene in a situation in which doctors believed there was no hope.

As the doctors surrounded Janie, I was in a real conundrum! My life was hanging by a thread. At that moment Janie had the power of life and death—*mine*—in her hands. No one but me knew that I was perfectly okay mentally and that my mind was clear.

The doctors were pressuring her to make a decission. Janie was classic in her response to the doctors. She said something like this: "You guys ought to be glad that I'm a Christ follower or I'd cuss you out royally right now! Not only is he not brain dead, but he's also going to recover from this situation. You'll see!"

At these words, the doctors shook their collective heads and turned and walked away. Janie says that they were muttering something about her "figuring it out soon enough." They were absolutely disrespectful to her. They had an inflated view of themselves and believed that they were infallible. I'm all for giving authority figures the respect that is due to them, but the truth is that we all make mistakes. It seems that we should walk with a degree of humility, because we can never tell when we are going to make a mistake in our advice. In my case, the advice that was given was almost disastrous.

It was frightening to hear the doctors talk about pulling the plug on me when I was fully cognizant and in charge of my wits. I ended up remaining in my coma for a couple of weeks, unable to do much more than blink. During that entire time, the doctors maintained that I had sustained significant brain damage. They ran tests on my brain to measure activity, but the tests were inconclusive. I just thank God that my wife had a heart to persevere, or I might well be a statistic at this point.

The Pain of Dehydration

Terri Schiavo died of thirst. Some experts like to say that she succumbed to starvation, but she actually died a slow and painful death due to dehydration.

Humans can carry on for weeks and weeks without food. I know a number of people who fasted for 50 days or longer, but during that time they had to stay hydrated. Terri Schiavo didn't have this choice—she was refused the relief of water in her mouth or intravenously during the last few days of her life. In fact, several times Terri's supporters tried to place a wet washcloth in her mouth. But they were ultimately prevented from offering her any form of relief.

Because of the nature of my injury, I also went with nothing but a wet Q-Tip placed on my tongue now and then. My colon was healing after a section of it was removed but couldn't sustain any liquids or food. Of all the pain I have experienced in life, nothing comes close to the pain of being dry in the mouth for 7 to 10 days. Even now I shudder when I remember the suffering that I went through.

Due to the lack of moisture, I developed large, open sores in my mouth and thick calluses on my tongue. The human body isn't designed to go without water; when it is withheld, great pain

results. Like Terri, I couldn't speak (I had a ventilator tube running down my throat), but I wept in pain and pleaded with my
eyes for water—just a little bit of water to quench my aching thirst.

At one point, I watched in utter dismay as some of the individuals involved with the Schiavo case assured the public that
Terri was dying peacefully and in absolute serenity without any
pain. I don't know where these people got their information, but
it was certainly not from firsthand experience. Dying of dehydration is one of the most drawn out and painful ways to succumb
imaginable. John 19:28 reports that it was part of the way that
Jesus died. The pain that I went through was beyond description.

The question that often comes up is whether Terri could feel
pain or was so far gone that she was beyond feeling anything. The
only qualified medical personnel that could correctly answer that
question are the neurologists who carefully examined her up close.
In Terri's case, these neurologists could not reach a consensus.

Could Terri feel pain? It seems likely. During the last couple
of weeks that she was in the hospice, she received morphine
every few hours. This fact was kept pretty quiet, but during a
news conference one of the representatives for the case let that
little fact slip. So the obvious question that comes up is why a
woman who was supposedly incapable of feeling any pain whatsoever would need morphine. It just doesn't add up.

I find it interesting that a pet has more rights in America
than a person like Terri Schiavo. If you or I tried to dehydrate or
starve a dog or cat to death, we would be arrested in a heartbeat.
Considering the pet-loving nature of America, we would likely
spend some time in jail.

Bamboozling

Let me be clear—Terri didn't die from her injuries. She could have
lived for years in her state of being. Her parents were willing to

support her financially and emotionally. They had plenty of resources to support her for decades to come. Again, the story just doesn't add up.

I know of a number of people who have dealt with situations similar to the Schiavo case. They experienced the trauma of having to make an executive decision for a close relative who didn't have a living will. I'm sure that cases such as these are currently being reviewed in all 50 states. What makes Terri's case unique, however, is that she wasn't dying of her injuries when her life support was cut off. In all the cases that I am aware of in which life support was terminated, the person was already dying—in fact, he or she was typically dying rapidly and painfully. In these instances, the family simply desired to speed up what God was obviously already doing in order to minimize suffering. In the Terri Schiavo case, our society crossed the line.

In an interview, Mel Gibson called Terri Schiavo's case bamboozling and warned that we will see worse than this in our society before long. I agree. This seems to be a case of the "frog in the kettle": If a frog is plunged into a kettle of hot water, it will immediately jump out; but if you start with cold water and gradually turn up the heat, the frog will actually stay in the kettle until it is boiled. The frog just doesn't notice the subtle degrees of increasing heat.

What will we see next? Death to the elderly who seem to be useless to society? A lack of caring about those who are sick or have deformities? Or will we see an all-out move to euthanize those who are deemed marginal and expendable?

The Quality of Life Argument

The "quality of life" card has been played over and over again in the Schiavo case. If I hear one more person use that term, I think I will barf. Since my accident, my quality of life has gone down significantly. I have daily bouts with colon problems that are incredibly troublesome. My legs are in a permanent weakened condition. My quadriceps are shot and my thigh muscles are non-existent—there is just skin on bone on both of my legs, which causes me to walk in a strange way. I can't do anything beyond a slow walk. I can't run, I can't jog, I can't hop and I can't play ball with my son. I'm always the last person to get off the plane. I have great difficulty swallowing pretty much anything due to the extended time I spent on the ventilator. I usually gag when I brush my teeth because my gag reflex has gone awry.

All of this equals a diminished quality of life. I'm glad those same doctors who thought that I was brain dead didn't have a deep philosophical discussion among themselves about my diminished quality of life. That might have given them more fuel for the fire to pull the plug on me. They had itchy fingers!

The diminished quality of life argument just doesn't float. This is especially true for Americans because we have no credibility. Approximately 80 percent of the people in the world have a low quality of life compared to the United States. We have a strange perspective regarding the quality of life issue in America. It's gotten to the point that we think if someone is stuck with a dial-up modem instead of broadband service, he or she must be suffering!

As I mentioned previously, after my accident I felt a strong desire to go to Mexico City and care for some of the people who lived in the city dumps. Teams from my church in Cincinnati now go to Mexico City several times per year. I still try to make it down there once a year as a form of reality therapy for my soul. These trips are simply life changing for the typically white, upper-middle-class folks who travel with us.

The people we care for actually spend their entire lives eking out a living in the filthy, stinking, insect-infested world of the city dumps. Hypodermic needles litter the ground, yet these trash-pickers walk around barefoot most of the time. I'm a germaphobe, so I feel a little insecure even walking around the place in thick-soled shoes. But these beautiful people forage over the dumps looking for materials that can be recycled.

Most of people we meet have tuberculosis. All of them have head lice. The people drink contaminated water and their lifespan is approximately 35 years, at best. None of them can read. The Mexican government doesn't want *gringos* like you and me to know about this situation because it's a black eye on Mexico as a whole. Our teams are barred from taking photos at most of the dump sites.

The children of the trash-pickers automatically follow their parents into this type of lifestyle. Here's my question: What kind of quality of life is that? It's obviously not much of a life to look forward to. Some of the children we run into don't even have names—that's how little intentionality there is to their lives. One eight-year-old boy that we met was simply called "Rabbit" because of his buckteeth. He had been abandoned in the dump by his parents, both of whom passed away a few years later of AIDS. We always bring him special gifts and clothes. He more or less fends for himself at the grand old age of eight!

We have been working to break the cycle of poverty, sickness and illiteracy at the dumps, but it is very difficult to lift the people's sights to something higher than their current condition. On top of that, organized crime receives a big percentage of the money these people do bring in, if you can believe that. There is a special place in hell for people like this who take advantage of the poor.

As Americans, we might find it surprising to note that these people are actually very happy with their lives. Many have come into a vital relationship with Christ over the past few years. They have their basic needs met as a result of a number of ministries that visit them on a regular basis. As Americans, we wouldn't be very happy living in those conditions. But these people don't know any different and are therefore quite satisfied.

The next time you hear some upper-middle-class person at a cocktail party arguing about the quality of life as it relates to the issue of living wills, just remember Rabbit at the city dump in Mexico City.

Writing a Living Will

I recommend that you draw up a living will to avoid having a Terri Schiavo-like situation with you or your spouse. Since my injury, I have been shocked into drawing up a living will.

You can write out your living will and officially leave it with your lawyer, or you can just put it on your computer's hard drive. Let your significant other know that you have made your wishes known in that document and that he or she can find it under "LivingWill.doc" or whatever else you have named it. If the time comes when this document is needed, your spouse can simply look it up. This document will suffice to make your wishes known.

In light of my harrowing experience, I decided to make a number of things clear. First, I want the medical staff around me to go to heroic efforts to save my life. I believe that it is possible for one to go into a coma and come out of it even after an extended period of time. Hey, it's happened before! I've said it before and I repeat my advice again here: Don't fall prey to the eagerness of the medical community to sign up for the "do not resuscitate" option. After experiencing a serious injury, coma, or any situation that doctors might call "hopeless," you could easily come back to a normal quality of life. If you get anything from reading this postscript, be encouraged to choose life!

In the case that I am declared brain-dead, I require that this declaration be attested to by the *team* of attending physicians (remember, I only go to big teaching hospitals now—no more little suburban hospitals for me!) as well as a named physician friend of mine. If all of these individuals agree that I have no brain activity, I then stipulate that doctors should disconnect me from life-giving machinery. If that machinery includes a feeding tube, I request that hospital personnel keep my mouth hydrated and apply balm on my lips. That may sound petty, but I want to minimize the suffering if there is any possibility that I could experience pain.

I explain in my living will that if my coma is unclear or moderate, I desire to be kept alive indefinitely. During that time, I want positive worship music to be played in my room several hours each day. I also want THE MESSAGE version of the Bible to be played near me. In addition, I want encouraging people to come to my room to visit and pray for me. I specifically clarify in my living will that I don't want negative doctors to be on my case and I never want them to speak negatively about my situation within earshot.

Terri Schiavo got us all thinking about our ultimate state of affairs. And that is a difficult thing to accomplish for Baby Boomers who still tend to think they are indestructible and just might live forever. Terri's life and passing will remain a matter of discussion and controversy for years to come. One thing seems for sure, however: God used the life of Terri Schiavo to get the attention of the world to focus on an issue that will most likely eventually impact all of our lives.

Note

1. This postscript was adapted from "Terri Schiavo: A Sister in Arms," *The Church Report*, May 2005. http://www.thechurchreport.com/content/view/379/32/. Used by permission.

THANKS

Janie Sjogren—You are my soul mate and my greatest editor. You know my "voice" better than anyone and can tell when I am writing well or just blowing smoke. Thanks for leveling with me, even when it's frustrating ("Write that an eighth time!"). You have been my best friend for almost 30 years. I know that the best is yet to come.

Dave Ping—I wouldn't have launched this book without your help, señor. You are a good friend and have the mind of a brilliant editor. Thanks for your many trips to my house to pump me up with ideas for how we could approach this story line. This has been my most difficult book to write, but you made it possible for me to finish it.

Dr. Doug Hanto—Thank you for being there for me on so many long nights when I was lying on the edge between life and death. I suspect that you went overboard for me like no other patient. You wept with me on more than one occasion. You have the heart of a healer. Thanks for being an amazing gift to me and to many, many others.

Steve Lawson—I asked God for Regal to appoint you as my editor. When I found out that you were appointed to this project, I felt that this book had a much greater possibility of being a success. Thanks for your friendship over the past 25 years. I hope to work on more books with you down the road.

The Regal Team—Bill Greig III, your vision and your prayers have encouraged me throughout this project. You are the ideal publisher. Mark Weising, thanks for sweating through the details, laughing at my jokes and caring enough to make this a better book. David Griffing, what can I say about the cover you designed—it is incredible! Rob Williams, we all need flexible people like you in our lives. Thank you for all your hard work and for getting this book to the printer on time.

OTHER BOOKS BY STEVE SJOGREN

Conspiracy of Kindness:
A Refreshing Approach to Sharing the Love
of Jesus with Others

Community of Kindness:
A Refreshing New Approach to Planting
and Growing a Church

Changing the World Through Kindness:
Living a Life That Will Change Your Family, Your City
and Eventually the World

Making a Good Church Great:
Becoming a Community God Calls Home

Steve Sjogren and his wife, Janie, have planted churches in Los Angeles, Baltimore, Cincinnati, Tampa, and in Oslo, Norway. Steve currently writes, speaks, and mentors church planters. He is the author of a number of books, including *Conspiracy of Kindness* and *Changing the World Through Kindness*, coauthor of *Community of Kindness*, and has written articles that have appeared in *Charisma, New Man, Discipleship Journal*, and more. Steve and Janie have three adult children.